THE INTERNATIONAL
MONETARY FUND

THE INTERNATIONAL MONETARY FUND

Retrospect and Prospect

BY

SHIGEO HORIE

President of the Bank of Tokyo

With a Foreword by

SIR ROY HARROD

NEW YORK
ST MARTIN'S PRESS INC
1964

MACMILLAN AND COMPANY LIMITED
St Martin's Street London WC2
also Bombay Calcutta Madras Melbourne

THE MACMILLAN COMPANY OF CANADA LIMITED
70 Bond Street Toronto 2

ST MARTIN'S PRESS INC
175 Fifth Avenue New York 10 NY

PRINTED IN GREAT BRITAIN

TO THE MEMORY
OF MY WIFE
MONICA AYAKO

CONTENTS

vii

FOREWORD

BY

SIR ROY HARROD

IT is with great pleasure that I write a foreword to this book by my friend, Mr. Shigeo Horie, President of the Bank of Tokyo, a man of great experience and learning, and of subtle intelligence.

From a purely utilitarian point of view I believe that this book will have an important part to play. As a tutor, I have found difficulty in advising adequate and up-to-date reading on the subject of the International Monetary Fund. I am sure that this volume will be welcomed on that account in many universities.

Mr. Horie opens with a retrospect of monetary history. There is much originality in his definition and analysis of the nature of the old gold standard system, which was centred upon London, and in the way in which he traces the stages in the decline of that system. He gives a very clear account of the genesis and development of the International Monetary Fund.

Japan has now been drawn into closer monetary relations with the western world by its membership of the 'Paris Club' and of the OECD; but until quite recently a Japanese observer necessarily viewed developments in these parts of the world with a certain detachment. This adds substantially to the value of Mr. Horie's work. He is well equipped with a scholarly knowledge of the progress of events. When assessing motives and in giving weight to various happenings, he sometimes makes points that will be novel to many English-speaking readers. Their interest in the book will thereby be kept lively.

At the time of writing, intensive study is being made of possibilities of reform in the world's monetary system. It is of interest that Mr. Horie, bringing his finely attuned mind to bear upon the present situation, is of the opinion that what I would describe as a rather far-reaching reform is needed. Thus his book is very timely.

AUTHOR'S PREFACE

SINCE the term 'crisis' was first used to describe the state of the world monetary system, there have been heated discussions in various quarters about the reform of the present International Monetary Fund system.

For many years I have been keenly interested in the Fund's organization, its character and operations, from both the practical and academic standpoints. I have availed myself of every opportunity to study it and I have been fortunate in having opportunities to absorb the atmosphere of international debate at the Fund's annual meetings. For this reason and others, I decided to publish my studies in book form with various data, new and old, and my experiences, as basic materials.

The idea of the Fund did not arise suddenly in the minds of those who took part in drafting and establishing it. As has been the case with all social phenomena, a very long time elapsed and tremendous efforts were exerted before the way was opened for its birth. The present system has its origin in the international gold standard system which was the first to embody an international monetary system. Further, the lessons learned in the field of international finance during the inter-war period and the experience gained in solving complex problems led up to its establishment.

In this book I first analyse the international gold standard system, and then trace the development and changes in it during the inter-war period. In this way I endeavour to help readers to grasp the process by which the Fund system was established. On the basis of my experience of what has gone before and an analysis of the present Fund arrangements, I survey various plans for reform and set out my views on its future prospects.

My conclusion, which may sound commonplace, is that currency should always be rigidly controlled, both internally and internationally, and that international control should be exclusively by an international institution. Fortunately, a trend toward closer international economic co-operation has been strengthening in recent years, and circumstances necessitate closer co-operation in future. I believe that this trend will increase and eventually lead to the establishment of as near an ideal system of international currency control as we can hope to get.

Since this work has been done in the little time I could spare from my busy bank life, I fear there may be some defects in my analysis; if so, I hope to remedy them with the help of my readers.

It is my pleasant duty to express my thanks for assistance of various kinds to my predecessors, and to fellow lecturers and professors, in the Economics Department of Tokyo University, my Alma Mater, at which I have been a lecturer for more than ten years. In fact it can be said that this work sees the light of day partly through my academic association with the University.

I owe a particular debt of gratitude to Professor Yoshitaro Wakimura, who helped me with much understanding and patience in the completion of my work. I am also grateful to Sir Roy Harrod, an outstanding economist, whom I always regard as my teacher, for his invaluable help in publishing my studies.

SHIGEO HORIE

10 September 1963

THE INTERNATIONAL GOLD STANDARD AND THE MULTILATERAL CREDIT AND SETTLEMENT SYSTEM

THE international gold standard was the first clear instance of an organized international monetary and financial system. However, it was not from the beginning designed as such. This 'universality' resulted from the adoption by many countries of the gold standard as their domestic monetary system. In this respect, it is remarkably different from the IMF, which from the beginning was meant to be an international monetary and financial system, albeit an artificial one. Moreover, the international gold standard system was in fact a system based upon the pound sterling, in other words, a British Pound Standard. This, as is well known, arose from the character of Britain's economy and its status in the world. Its institution owed its existence, however, to the great development and perfection of a foreign exchange system. Already in the nineteenth century and thereafter, Britain was making remarkable progress in the field of foreign exchange which, together with confidence in the stabilized character of the pound backed by gold, prepared the ground for its assumption of the role of an international currency.[1]

The historical fact that the pound became a new international currency must be regarded as an 'exceptional state of affairs',[2] for it was supported by a number of exceptional economic conditions.

For instance, there was the basic reality that Britain for a

[1] The beginnings of a foreign exchange system appeared earlier on the continent than in England. Though it existed to a considerable extent on the continent in the latter half of the sixteenth century, it only began to flourish in England in the latter half of the seventeenth century. Following the industrial revolution, however, the commercial centre moved from the continent to London, and, as a result, the system came to be readjusted and firmly established there by the beginning of the nineteenth century. It was about the middle of that century that London consolidated its position as a centre of international finance.

[2] League of Nations, *International Currency Experience*, 1944, p. 195.

time held a practical monopoly as the manufacturers for the world above all other nations, but institutionally, we cannot ignore the following two exceptional factors.

Firstly, Britain was the first country to adopt a gold standard system and it did so in a distinctive fashion.

The adoption of the gold standard system in Britain came about through the introduction in 1816 of the golden sovereign as unrestricted legal tender, its basis being later strengthened by the Bank Charter Act of 1844. The pound had a number of uncomfortable experiences, particularly during the currency confusion that occurred during the Napoleonic Wars and the financial panics that were frequent during the following fifty years. The Parliamentary committees that enquired into these events have left much material and many reports which are invaluable sources.

Thus, while other West European countries on the continent still remained in the era of gold and silver bimetallism, Britain increased her knowledge of the gold standard, and acquired both the techniques and skill in operating it.[1]

Further, the pound was freely convertible into gold, at a certain specific weight of gold, and was used without restriction for foreign payments. Other countries, however, had only a pseudo form of the gold standard, always subject to some restrictions. For example, the sale of gold for export purposes was generally controlled by the authorities concerned, and, in many cases, these authorities reserved the right to conversion through media other than gold (*i.e.* silver).

Another unique feature in Britain's favour was the London gold market. The sale and purchase of gold and its export and import were quite freely permitted. Sterling creditors could obtain and take away as much gold as they needed, while debtors could make shipments of gold to London in payment of their debts. Those who possessed gold were always able to obtain other currencies in exchange through both gold bullion and exchange transactions. If, therefore, there had been no such facilities supplementing the conversion operations of the central bank, it is very doubtful whether gold shipments under the international gold standard system would have functioned smoothly.

[1] Bank for International Settlements, *The Sterling Area*, 1953, p. 8.

Merchants and traders in foreign countries wishing to sell or buy gold in such central markets as London had to have recourse to such media of credit as a foreign bill of exchange. This they did by drawing bills on the sterling funds to their credit, and obtaining gold or, conversely, by shipping and selling gold and thus obtaining funds in sterling. When, therefore, there were large sales of gold abroad there resulted a decrease in the sterling funds available with a rise in the rate of the pound in consequence; but when, on the contrary, there were large purchases of gold from overseas, an increase in the amount of sterling funds resulted, with a decline in the rate of the pound on the foreign exchange market. In this way, the market price of gold and the sterling rate of exchange became interdependent; but so long as the Bank of England was willing to sell or buy gold freely at a fixed price, the market price of gold remained stable.[1]

This meant that in London the entry and exit of gold through open market transactions was quite free, thereby supplementing the central bank's function of conversion, and, as a result, the shipment of gold at export or import point worked perfectly. In other countries, however, no free transactions in gold were permitted, except the so-called 'one way gold market'. This allowed only the purchase of gold by the country concerned.[2] This difference in operating enhanced the credit of the pound and, in turn, formed the basic condition for ensuring the stability of international exchange.

The second factor was international finance which was facilitated by Britain. International settlement and international finance constitute the two sides of one and the same function, and in order to facilitate the active use of the pound by other countries, with London as the centre of exchange settlement, it was necessary to provide these countries with external credit.

The building up of short-term credit based on the pound is effected by the acceptance and discount of foreign bills of exchange. The action of accepting a bill means that one

[1] In this connection, however, it should be remembered that though the gold shipping cost remains the same, no matter whether it is sold to or bought from the Bank of England or on the open market, the gold points will undergo some change.

[2] H. E. Evitt, *A Manual of Foreign Exchange*, 1960, 5th ed., p. 48.

whose credit is high lends part of it to another whose credit is low. Therefore, one who has been granted credit is able to have his bill discounted as a fine bank bill at a more favourable rate than if he relied exclusively on his own credit.

On the international plane, a bank or business firm which is capable of providing such credit must enjoy high status and credit abroad, and British banks and firms happened to be in such a position. This fact gave rise to an active bill acceptance business, and brought into existence the acceptance house and merchant banker.[1]

This method of finance through acceptance of bills obtained not only for trade with Britain but also for trade between third countries. Thus was created what is known as the London acceptance credit, under which a bill of exchange drawn under letter of credit is accepted and discounted by those financial institutions which were established in London, and such borrowers were able to take advantage of the rates of interest ruling on the London financial market.

As the excellence of London as a centre of international finance became firmly established, short-term funds from various foreign countries tended increasingly to be concentrated there, part becoming deposits with discount houses, which, in turn, served as the source of further external finance.

In this way the development of the bill acceptance business accompanied the development of the discounting business, and the discount market came to play a very important role within the ramifications of Britain's financial operations. As a result, the term 'money and discount market' became widely used. But however excellent that mechanism is, a rise in the rate of interest reduces the value of its use. If, therefore, money market rates of interest rise in step with an increase in Bank Rate, then foreign debtors tend to remit funds to London to clear their debts at maturity, and foreign financial institutions are inclined to transfer any available funds in their possession to benefit from the high interest rates in force. Thus a change in rates is immediately followed by the inflow

---

[1] In London, at that time, exchange banks in general laid emphasis upon acceptance business for trade within the British Commonwealth, whereas acceptance houses attached importance to finance between the Commonwealth and other foreign countries.

of short-term funds which tend to improve the balance of payments position and prevent the outflow of gold. In Britain, therefore, the interest rate policy of the central bank has tended to have more speedy and precise effects than elsewhere.[1]

The above remarks are chiefly concerned with short-term finance, which, however, when supplemented by long-term finance and the capital market, made it possible to build up an international trade and to establish a healthy system of international finance with London as its centre. In this way the adjustment of credit through gold, which is the original and essential function of a gold standard system, came to be achieved on the basis of centralization in London, and the rationalization of world economy through gold was brought into being.

[1] W. M. Dacey, *The British Banking Mechanism*, pp. 58-9.

II

THE INTERNATIONAL GOLD
STANDARD SYSTEM AND FOREIGN
EXCHANGE RATES

THE international gold standard system owed a great deal to
the fixed rate system in its ability to preserve the unity of
currency in the world economy.

The currency of any given country under the gold standard
system was convertible into gold both within that country and
externally, and not only into gold but also into the currencies
of other countries at virtually a fixed rate, and in that respect
the currency of any country on the gold standard became an
international currency just like gold itself. It could even be
said that in practice, though not nominally, the currencies of
all countries were a single currency based upon gold. Indeed,
the word 'convertibility' was used at that time in just that sense.

The reason why the phrase 'at virtually a fixed rate' is
used above is that there existed other free gold markets with
fluctuating rates, as in London, and foreign exchange rates
were able to and did fluctuate within the gold points. Thus, if
the central bank were willing to buy or sell gold at a single
fixed rate, then transactions would, in practice, be limited to
those with the central bank; but if the central bank were
prepared to quote different rates for buying and for selling,
scope would be given for market transactions.[1]

And as any medium of credit (for example, foreign
exchange) expressed in any of the currencies of countries on
the gold standard is based upon gold, a gap may arise between

[1] Before 1932, the Treasury Department of the United States agreed to the
purchase and sale of gold at the fixed rate of $20.67183 an ounce of fine gold and,
therefore, there was no scope for the establishment of a gold market.
In Britain, however, the Bank of England was under the obligation (a) of
delivering gold coins at par (under the Resumption Act of 1819), viz. the equivalent
of 1 standard ounce in exchange for notes (and token coins) worth £3 17s. 10½d.,
and (b) of buying gold bullion at the price of £3 17s. 9d. a standard ounce (under
the Bank Charter Act of 1844). (R. S. Sayers, *Bank of England Operations*, 1890–
1914, pp. 71-4.)

supply and demand which can easily be adjusted by moving gold to the central market where there is a greater demand for the currency concerned. This, briefly, is what is meant by the gold points.

Besides, apart from the settlement of current transactions, there are always speculators operating in the money market looking for opportunities to make a profit through arbitrage, and where the difference in the rates between markets is large, they are sure to operate for margins, with the result that the imbalance is rectified and the close inter-relation between the markets is restored. Thus, if a resident in country A wants to buy gold in country B, he obtains the currency of country B by selling the currency of country A, and then, if he sells this gold in country C, he can obtain the currency of that country. To complete the operation, he then sells the currency of country C so that he may convert it into the currency of country A, his own country. If, however, it is impossible for some reason to effect the conversion from the currency of country C to that of country A, he would again have to pass through the currency of country B or through the currency of yet another country altogether.

In order to engage in arbitrage transactions of this nature, the operator must be well versed not only in the movement of the price of gold in countries A and C and in the trend of exchange rates in various other financial centres but he must also operate astutely. For that purpose, he should have access to a wide range of information and be possessed of a high degree of specialized technique. If arbitrage transactions of this nature are undertaken on a large scale, they will presumably greatly affect the market prices of gold and of exchange rates. As, however, such operations spread the pressure of demand and supply over several markets, they may well have the effect of stabilizing the various rates in the markets concerned. Under the gold standard system, therefore, not only is the scope for fluctuation in the rates narrow, but also the fluctuations themselves are inevitably limited by the skill and expertise of the exchange dealers. In fact, this kind of fluidity is one of the functions of a free market.

That the pound, which was the principal currency under the international gold standard system, ensured stability among the currencies of other nations, should be attributed not merely to the settled character of the pound itself, but more particularly to the perfect freedom to engage in arbitrage transactions in gold or foreign exchange.[1]

It is certainly true, however, that under the gold standard system it was the free import and export of gold which was the final check upon the fluctuation of exchange rates at a time of imbalance of external payments. In other words, as the gold standard system had fixed exchange rates, the movement of gold became necessary. In this sense, a country's gold reserves created a buffer against the outside world.

These movements of gold had another side. They led to fluctuations of business activity.

Under any gold standard system, the outflow of gold contracts the supply of credit and thereby applies a brake to economic activities; on the other hand, an inflow expands the basis of credit, thus stimulating economic activities. The reason for this is that under the gold standard system, gold reserves serve not only as an external buffer but also as a reserve against the issue of currency and, consequently, closely combine the domestic and external sides of a country's economy into one whole. In this way, under the gold standard system, the trend of business in one country spreads to another, which, as a rule, does nothing to counteract this influence. As a result, a high degree of synchronization takes place in commodity prices, national income and business activity in the countries concerned, which they regard it as the rule of the game not to obstruct.

Thus, the fixed exchange rate served as an immovable base, around which the other factors had to fluctuate. Moreover, the amount of gold used for currency by the whole world was adequate and the scale of credit was controlled by it.

Under a free and unrestrained economy, however, planning on an international scale is non-existent, and the domestic credit policies of all countries have been subject to its vagaries. This is certainly the greatest drawback of a free economy, under which 'the scope for independent domestic action is

[1] R. F. Harrod, *The Pound Sterling*, 1952. (Translated into Japanese by the Research Department of the Bank of Tokyo and, under the title of *Gendai-no-Pondo*, published by the Shiseido, Tokyo, p. 4.)

extremely narrow. Exchange rates are stabilized at the expense of giving up all other possible aims of monetary management such as economic stabilization and full employment.' [1]

Why, then, did no country show any strong opposition to being engulfed in a world system such as is described above? It is reasonable to suppose that there were many contributory factors, but there can be little doubt that the following four were the most important.

The first was elasticity in the economy. Prices correctly reflected the relation between demand and supply, and the adaptation of the economy to the price change was swift, thus speedily creating a new balance. Under such conditions, the effects of a price change are immediately absorbed by adaptations made by the domestic economy.

The second was the rising importance of capitalism, owing to which the problem of employment in the past did not present so grave a question as in the present century, and the conflict between world and national economies in this respect was not serious. It is generally recognized that this second factor was a fundamental condition for the harmonious development of world economy.

The third was the increasing production of gold, which made it possible for credit to expand in step with the development of world economy, and at the same time ensured a sufficiency of gold and prevented a decline in liquidity. [2]

In this way, the price of gold was stabilized for more than a century, and the gold parity of the pound established by Newton in 1717 was maintained without a hitch except during the Napoleonic and First World wars: this was indeed deserving of the description 'an outstanding achievement'.

The fourth factor was balance in the world economy. It is a well-known fact that apart from the self-balancing operation of the gold standard system, this balance was maintained by the special position occupied by Britain at the hub of world economy. The fact is especially noteworthy that the gold

---

[1] G. N. Halm, *International Monetary Co-operation*, 1945, p. 21.

[2] About the middle of the nineteenth century, the amount of gold produced was increased by the gold produced in the United States, and when this source showed signs of falling production, the gold mines in South Africa during the 1880s much more than filled the gap.

absorbed by Britain in its current transactions was in turn widely distributed through its external investments and did not result in its concentration as came to be the case in later years.

Here the question arises as to whether or not this harmonious balance in the world economy under the gold standard system was left entirely to such fortuitous conditions as are mentioned above, or to the self-adjusting action of the gold points. Actually, as was stated in the last chapter, in London, which acted as the centre of a common economic bloc under the gold standard, the discount policy of the central bank operated more satisfactorily and effectively than under the floating exchange rate system. What, then, are the factors that brought about such a situation?

It is clear that the stabilized value of a currency tied to gold definitely fixes the point at which interest arbitrage is profitable and brings about a balanced movement of funds. The absence of exchange risks, however, at the same time prevents the development of a forward exchange system. So long as there is a fixed limit for a fluctuation in rates, there can be no question of an exchange rate going beyond that limit. The necessity of an exchange contract was not so well recognized. Under the gold standard system, therefore, there was, generally speaking, no systematized forward exchange market. The principle of interest parity under which the gap between spot and forward exchange rates showed the difference between interest rates was not then in operation.

If, however, the gold standard system ceases to function, resulting in the values of all currencies fluctuating without limits, then the difference in interest rates ceases to be the only basis for the movement of funds. Thus in addition to the interest charge there would be the cost of covering the risk of exchange, which extra charge would tend to reduce the flow of capital seeking a profitable turn in another market than its own. The inflow would cease before it reached the total which would be required to cover the gap on current account.

In addition, the absence of a profitable basis prevents the movement of long-term capital. However, it would activate the international movement of those funds which desired to escape from countries with unestablished currencies or of those which sought a speculative profit taking advantage of the fluctuation of exchange rates but lacking a commercial basis, while those funds which sought a profitable basis would be subject to the disadvantage of the interest parity as a result of the swap operation.

III

CHANGES IN AND COLLAPSE
OF THE INTERNATIONAL
GOLD STANDARD SYSTEM

Section 1.—The Gold Exchange Standard System

IT is difficult to be precise as to when the international gold standard system began to crumble. It may be said, however, to have worked smoothly until just before the outbreak of the First World War in 1914. During and after the war, convertibility into gold was universally suspended for a time, but there was a strong inclination everywhere to return to the system. There was, however, a steadily growing atmosphere which tended to stifle the automatic functioning of the system.

There was a disinclination to give priority to external interests, which, though it was the most serious drawback of the gold standard system, yet, ensured the stability of international exchange.

The first of the four factors mentioned in the preceding chapter, that is, the adaptation of the economy to the changes in prices, began to show signs of not working smoothly, and, in consequence, pressures on the economy from abroad were not capable of being easily absorbed at home. It was only natural, therefore, that the authorities concerned should seek to resist this tendency by putting up barriers to these external influences, or to eliminate them as rapidly as possible. In addition, the prevailing wave of economic nationalism tended to consider employment and national income as the primary objects of economic stabilization, and to give only secondary consideration to the level of commodity prices.

For example, the United States, which experienced a great inflow of gold following the war, adopted a tight credit policy, thereby disregarding its favourable gold reserves through fear of an over-heated economy and its consequences. This meant a regulated dollar instead of one controlled by gold, which was a policy of giving priority to domestic stabilization.

Prior to this, inflationary policies during the war had exercised wide and profound effects upon the economies of all countries. In the field of currency, there were many changes as mentioned below.

First, Britain and many other countries adopted a policy of centralizing gold, thus increasing considerably the gold reserves of their central banks. However, inflation during the war resulted in a great increase in the amount of paper money in circulation,[1] and it was impossible to meet the demand for conversion at home. Their gold reserves, therefore, were used solely for the maintenance of external convertibility.

Secondly, the international imbalances of payments in wartime and the mushrooming of economically weak countries, which became independent after the war, brought about an international maldistribution of gold. In addition, rising production costs resulted in a decline in the output of gold, so that a shortage of gold was keenly felt by all.[2]

Thirdly, in order to maintain their gold standard system, no matter however imperfectly, and to continue to produce under such conditions, there was no other course than to resort to a dollar standard system and have recourse to abundant dollar funds. And so it is today.

Under such conditions it was only natural that the current attempt at the restoration of a gold standard system should be directed toward an economy in the use of gold rather than toward a gold coin standard system, which had been in existence in former days.

At the International Financial Conference held at Brussels (Conférence Financière Internationale, Bruxelles) in 1920, this feeling had been manifest, but at the Genoa Conference it assumed a greater significance, since the resolutions adopted

[1] During the First World War, with almost no reserves, Britain issued currency notes as well as bank notes under the Currency and Bank Note Act, 1914.

[2] The amount of gold produced in the world decreased by about one-third during the years from 1915 to 1922, and its pre-war level was not reached for some time.

Moreover, following the world-wide deflation from 1920 to 1922, the view was generally held by experts that the shortage of gold would bring about chronic deflation. (R. F. Harrod, *The Pound Sterling*, Japanese edition published by the Shiseido under the title of *Gendai-no-Pondo*, p. 12.)

at that conference proposed (*a*) that a return be made to a gold standard system,[1] (*b*) that gold should not necessarily be insisted upon as part (or all) of the reserves, and (*c*) that, if possible, one of the participating countries should establish a free gold market in which any participating country could freely buy and sell exchange (gold exchange) on another participating country at a certain limit around exchange parity. These resolutions would have led to the conclusion of an international convention on the basis of a gold exchange standard.[2]

'Assets other than gold as reserves' mean external balances, bills, short-term securities or other suitable liquid assets which constitute claims on other participating countries, while those participating countries should fundamentally be on a gold standard or nearly so.

The idea of such a gold exchange system with gold exchange reserves was not entirely new, as, according to Professor Nurkse, a similar concept could be found in a system for regulating domestic exchange in Britain in the latter half of the eighteenth century, and in the 1880s and 1890s many countries subscribed to somewhat similar conventions. Even prior to 1914, in those countries which had adopted a gold standard system it was a common practice for a central bank to hold a certain amount of foreign exchange in addition to gold. In 1913, fifteen central banks in Europe together held reserves other than gold of about 12 per cent of their gold reserves, and in 1925, twenty-four central banks in Europe held about 27 per cent of their total reserves in assets other than gold.[3] It was also a noteworthy fact that less advanced countries such as India had already adopted such a system before the First World War.

In Britain, which had been the principal country on the gold standard system, the Committee on Currency and Foreign Exchange, commonly called the Cunliffe Committee, appointed in 1918, proposed a policy of deflation in order to return to a gold standard system. This idea was taken over in 1924 by the Committee on the Currency and Bank of

[1] 'Gold is the sole common standard that should now be adopted by every European country.' (Genoa International Conference, Currency Resolution 5.)
[2] League of Nations, *International Currency Experience*, 1944, p. 28.
[3] *Ibid.* p. 29.

England Note Issues, best known as the Bradbury Committee, which recommended the lifting of the gold embargo. However, the Cunliffe Committee made it clear in its interim report that the circulation of gold coins was not an essential element of the gold standard system, and that the centralization of the gold reserve in the central bank was more economical. The Bradbury Committee similarly decided that convertibility into gold coins was not essential, that it was in the nature of a luxury and that therefore it was inadvisable at least for the time being.

Britain adopted this course fearing that with the existing shortage of gold the large imports of gold required to put gold coins into circulation would exercise pressure upon the external value of the pound. Britain thus felt it advisable to economize in gold. For this reason, therefore, on its return to a gold standard in 1925, it was provided that,

(*a*) though the gold embargo was to be lifted, the prohibition of conversion into gold coins would remain, and the minting of such coins would be limited;

(*b*) in order to provide gold for export, the Bank of England should be under the obligation of selling gold bullion of over 400 ounces at the official price of £3 17s. 10½d. in exchange for legal tender.

Britain, in this way, adopted a gold bullion standard system.

Under this new system, gold reserves were regarded as necessary solely for external purposes, and it was therefore only from an international standpoint that it could be called a gold standard system. The gold exchange standard systems of other countries had much the same character, but in a more pronounced degree. As their currencies were no longer international as under the original gold standard system, the stability of their external value depended almost entirely upon a guarantee by the monetary authorities of their conversion into an international currency.[1]

As was said by Sir Winston Churchill, British Chancellor of the Exchequer at that time, such a system could rightly be called an 'international gold standard system'.

[1] Robert Triffin, *Gold and Dollar Crisis*, 1960, p. 65.

A currency system must have a character similar to that of the above-mentioned gold bullion standard to function smoothly as an international mechanism. As already pointed out, even under the original gold standard system, Britain alone had a gold standard in the strict sense of the term, the system in other countries having imperfections of some kind or other. In what way was the difference evident? It was shown in the sphere of external conversion into gold. A country which heads a group of gold exchange currency countries and freely allows external conversion into gold, should have either a gold coin standard system or a gold bullion standard system; and the other gold exchange countries would only have to be in possession of the currency of that principal country, to be on the gold exchange system. In this sense, the gold standard system is intrinsically an international system, embodying the essential elements of gold exchange.

What then is the most important difference between the original gold standard and the gold exchange standard system?

It lies in the fact that gold exchange is not gold itself, but only an external claim for gold.

Put in another way, gold exchange is nothing but foreign exchange, and, from the standpoint of international settlement, must be considered as an intermediate stage in the final settlement through gold. Any country which holds gold exchange has a right at any time to claim a final settlement in gold against the gold standard country concerned. When, however, a country does not claim a final settlement, but retains the claim in the form of foreign exchange, it is holding a credit which is redeemable against the gold standard country concerned. As a result, even if the central gold standard country sells gold exchange to any other participating country, it does not affect the gold reserves of that gold standard country. On the other hand, the participating country which has received the gold exchange can, against this reserve, create a further issue of currency.

In this way, if a gold standard country be regarded as a banking institution, a claim (that is, gold exchange) held by any other participating country against that gold standard country may be compared to a deposit, and the gold reserves held by it as a reserve against payment of that deposit; and, so long as confidence in its currency remains, it is hardly likely that there would be a 'run' on the whole of the deposits. It is therefore not necessary for the gold standard country to be in possession of 100 per cent gold reserves.

This leads to the conclusion that such a system, if run properly, would make it possible for the whole group to possess a very high rate of international liquidity although having a comparatively small amount of gold reserves. Herein lie the advantages of an economy in gold. Once, however, errors are committed, there would arise the danger of a crisis in the entire system of international currency.

Section 2.—Collapse of the Gold Standard System

The gold exchange standard system was adopted by many countries from the time Britain adopted a gold bullion standard system until it abandoned the system, that is, from about 1925 to about 1931.

The central bank of a country in adopting the system changes its articles of association, to give itself the power of holding foreign exchange in place of gold as a legal reserve. During the ten-year period from 1922 to 1931, some twenty-six central banks took such powers and many countries adopted the system, although they had no central bank.[1]

Thus, the percentage of foreign exchange reserves of twenty-four central banks in Europe, which stood at twenty-seven in 1925, rose to forty-two in 1928.[2]

Opinions vary as to the causes of the collapse of the system. The view that carried most weight was that it was highly imprudent of Britain to return to a gold standard at the old parity after the war without adequate preparation, and that this was the fundamental cause of the collapse of the system.

It was due fundamentally to its long tradition of political economy that Britain hastened to restore its gold standard system. This was expressed by R. S. Sayers as follows:

'A long tradition in English political economy lies behind the view that any tampering with the monetary unit is a fraud

---

[1] League of Nations, *International Currency Experience*, 1944, p. 30.
[2] *Ibid.* p. 29.

on either debtors or creditors. The Ricardian view was that the nation had decided, and decided rightly, that the value of the monetary unit should be made to depend upon the world value of gold, and that the supply of money should be so closely tied to conditions in the market for gold that there should be no room for human manipulation, however well intended. Any discretionary action would be "tinkering with currency".'[1]

Apart from that tradition, it is undeniable that Britain was unmindful of the fact that although it had adopted a fairly strong deflationary policy before its return to a gold standard system, it could not achieve adequate adjustment at home, and that its gold standard mechanism of former days had been supported by many extraneous factors. This point was also brought out by Sayers:

'The ultimate answer to Bagehot's problem was the clear one of a powerful bank rate weapon with a "thin film of gold". It is difficult now (and apparently it was impossible in 1918) to remember how new it still was in 1914, and how dependent it was upon a conjunction of circumstances that might easily — and did — pass away.'[2]

The fundamental cause of the collapse of the gold standard system, as has already been explained, lies in the fact that though elasticity in the economy was gradually lost, a system was re-instituted which required that very elasticity as its most necessary element. It is also an undeniable fact that the drawbacks inherent in the gold exchange standard system and the violation of its rules played no small part in its downfall. What were the circumstances that led to its collapse?

The first was concerned with the gold exchange reserves themselves.

At that time, many countries were receiving stabilization or reconstruction loans chiefly from Britain and the United States, and parts of these were concentrated in the hands of their central banks. The credits thus obtained were suddenly withdrawn owing to the liquidity panic in 1931, a step which was one of the causes of the system's collapse.[3]

---

[1] R. S. Sayers, *Central Banking after Bagehot*, pp. 1-2.
[2] *Ibid.* p. 18.
[3] League of Nations, *International Currency Experience*, 1944, p. 64.

Furthermore, in general the gold exchange countries were intent upon improving their international balances of payments and made energetic efforts to obtain gold exchange. Some countries, to achieve this objective, resorted to a deflationary policy to lower prices and production costs, while others kept their exchange rates at levels that led to their currencies being undervalued. These measures caused bullish speculation from abroad, leading to an inflow of foreign currency.[1]

On the other hand, such moves led the gold standard countries to increase their efforts for the protection of their gold reserves. These efforts were also furthered by the following factors.

Generally speaking, the composition of gold exchange holdings differed from country to country, and the principal gold standard countries found it difficult to obtain information on the total of these short-term liabilities. (If reserves had been limited to the current accounts at central banks bearing no interest, the picture would have been quite different.)

Countries were, therefore, compelled to make every effort to protect their gold reserves against potential demands for gold. It was chiefly owing to this external factor that from 1925 Britain adopted a deflationary policy. Indeed, it was, as Dr. Feliks Mlynarski says,[2] a gold sterilization policy in another form.

The policy adopted by the United States of America also had the same purpose.

These policies gave rise to serious imbalances at home, and, as in Britain, caused difficulties with labour.

That all countries showed such enthusiasm for the possession of gold exchange was due to the fact that not only were they under the necessity of economizing gold, but were also saved the cost of shipment, as would have been the case in transferring gold; and, in addition, they were attracted by the opportunity of profitable investment.

The efforts of all countries were therefore directed towards the expansion of short-term credits with the central gold

---

[1] *Ibid.* p. 32.
[2] League of Nations, *The Functioning of the Gold Standard* (by Dr. Feliks Mlynarski), 1931, pp. 20-1.

standard countries. According to Sir Roy Harrod, in London, though little notice was taken of it at the time, traders showed a growing preference for holding sterling balances for making settlements rather than by utilizing the credit provided by bank acceptances.[1]

This tendency, in turn, gave rise to the following results :

(*a*) First of all, it became possible for the principal countries universally to obtain short-term credits. With these credits as a basis, they could expand credit provided domestically. Thus the way was opened for short-term borrowing and long-term lending. Short-term credits of this nature are never withdrawn from the principal countries so long as they are working balances but only move from the account of one country to the account of another. The effect, therefore, is to provide the principal countries with long-term credits. As, however, such credits are inherently of a short-term nature, there was no knowing when and for what reason they would be withdrawn. Besides, as it was very difficult for the principal countries to make this distinction clearly, they were naturally obliged to resort to borrowing on a short-term and lending on a long-term basis almost unconsciously. Such a procedure was all very well so long as things went smoothly, but, once a global financial crisis occurred, short-term credits would be withdrawn across the board, as was experienced by Britain, while long-term loans would become uncollectable, thus leaving the principal countries in an unenviable position.

(*b*) Further, the accumulation of gold exchange, while strengthening the power of the commercial banks, had the effect of weakening the credit-controlling functions of a central bank. That is, with the increasing trend of commercial banks to hold foreign currency accounts, the external reserves of a country are spread among the banks, unless exchange control can achieve a concentration of exchange. Not only is this so, but those commercial banks which hold such accounts are able to use them for the expansion of their own lending. This leads to the danger of the central bank of the country concerned being incapable of exercising control over the extent of the credit expansion or over the conditions on which it is granted.

[1] R. F. Harrod, *The Pound Sterling*, as translated into Japanese under the title *Gendai-no-Pondo*, and published by the Shiseido, p. 12.

From 1927 to 1929 the United States of America experienced an inflow of an enormous amount of funds from gold exchange countries, resulting in a boom on the stock market which made the reaction that came later so much greater. The Federal Reserve System, however, was unable to take any effective measure against it.

Secondly, the gold exchange standard system exerted an anomalous influence upon the gold market. Under the gold standard system, all those countries which possessed only a limited amount of foreign currency could only obtain it by selling their own currencies for gold. In other words, the action of buying gold unavoidably influenced the exchange market. On the other hand, under the gold exchange standard system it was possible to buy gold with no effects whatever upon the exchange market, so long as there were foreign currency holdings.

Furthermore, the central banks of gold exchange standard countries had only to sell gold exchange for the purpose of adjusting exchange rates, without the necessity of selling gold; hence, they seldom appeared as sellers of gold, though they might be buyers. The result was that (a) the organic relation between the gold market and the foreign exchange market, which existed under the gold standard system, disappeared, and (b) the central banks in all countries found it possible so to operate the market that they could effect arbitrage transactions favourable to themselves.

As an example, commercial banks in Germany purchased a considerable quantity of gold in London in the autumn of 1928, and it might be supposed that as the result the loss of sterling by those German banks would have been favourable to the London exchange rates. In fact, however, the Reichsbank at the time repeatedly provided the commercial banks with their own sterling funds and, therefore, the sterling rate did not reach its gold export point. The possibility had arisen of a prolonged continuation of a movement of gold in only one direction owing to arbitrage; moreover, the sterling exchange held by the Reichsbank at that time came from credits created in Germany's favour.[1]

---

[1] League of Nations, *The Functioning of the Gold Standard* (by Dr. Feliks Mlynarski), 1931, pp. 21-2.

The same thing may be said of France, which had also been converting foreign currency holdings into gold, but had finally refrained from doing so in consideration of the monetary difficulties in other countries (especially Britain). Commenting on this, Professor Nurkse states that from the very beginning France was lukewarm towards a gold exchange system; its partial adoption was only a makeshift measure, but its real intention was to give an 'exclusively metallic foundation' to its own currency.[1]

Prior to this France had recorded a large surplus in its balance of payments owing to the withdrawal of its own capital investments from abroad and the fall in the exchange rate; but the fate of the gold exchange standard system was practically decided when it decided to accept only gold in settlement.[2]

The gold reserves of the Bank of England at that time were maintained at a level of about £150 million. That level, however, was barely maintained by the inflow of gold from its colonies and by new production. The gold market was affected by the activities of unidentified buyers, resulting in a rapid increase in the volume of transactions.[3]

Thirdly, under a system which necessitates adjustments being made by media other than gold, it is highly desirable that one of the group of countries concerned should operate a gold centre to which all the others are tied. At that time, however, such a centre was not restricted to one place, for in addition to Britain, France adopted a gold bullion standard from 1928, and the United States of America also continued to accept conversion into gold. Thus the gold centre was divided amongst London, Paris and New York.

[1] League of Nations, *International Currency Experience*, 1944, p. 39.
In this connection, it should be remembered that up to June 1928, France was in practice on the gold standard system and used it fully, for the purpose of strengthening the franc, but as a result of the currency reform of the above date, came to adopt a gold exchange system.   [2] *Ibid.*
[3] League of Nations, *The Functioning of the Gold Standard*, 1931, p. 23.
According to this book, the amount of gold bought and sold by the Bank of England in the years listed below was (unit: £1 million):

Year	Purchased	Sold
1925	17·2	28·8
1926	24·0	17·7
1927	19·4	20·7
1928	35·6	36·9
1929	52·7	60·9

Further, the operation of such a group requires, more than anything else, co-operation among the participating countries, as had already been suggested by the protocol of the Genoa Conference, and close co-operative action in all three centres. However, there was no indication whatever of such co-operation even being attempted. Thus the world's currency system, which should have been characterized by stability and co-operation among nations, proved to be a medium in which countries strove with one another for the possession of gold, leaving no hope for such a system to last for very long.

For this reason a proposal was later made that the gold exchange standard system should remedy its shortcomings and be run along more rational lines. It aimed first of all at securing international co-operation, and then at concentrating at one centre all gold exchange reserves which are apt to be dispersed, and at limiting the number of those institutions authorized to hold them. This idea underwent a further development later when the Gold Committee of the League of Nations, by way of giving a practical turn to materializing its so-called 'intelligent collaboration', advanced the contention that the gold exchange reserves of all countries should be entrusted to such an international organization as the Bank for International Settlements (BIS), and that that international organization should entrust its deposits to the central banks of the participating countries. These ideas and recommendations can be said to have been the germ of the IMF system of later days.

Section 3.—Exchange Stabilization Funds and the Tripartite Monetary Agreement

The change in the gold standard system, explained in Section 2, was a process of development from an automatic gold standard to an artificially controlled gold standard system. It was also a change from the gold standard system itself to a controlled currency system, under which the basis of currency was gradually released from gold. When this controlled gold standard system became impossible to maintain, certain changes took place in the field of international finance.

First, gold, though it had lost its role as domestic currency, retained its position as a medium of final settlement in international transactions.

In this way the international currency system was, as was stated by Nurkse, moving towards an 'international gold settlement system'.[1] But in order that the system should operate smoothly, a strict control of gold, to be carried out with international co-operation, was necessary, wherever its centre may have been; but at first this was lacking.

Secondly, under the bank note standard system, in sharp contrast to the working of the gold standard system, the level of commodity prices at home became the axis on which exchange rates fluctuated in an unstable manner. So long as each country stuck to its policy of giving priority to commodity prices or to the level of employment at home, this was inevitable.

Though the international movement of gold was in many cases prohibited, this did not lead to the abolition of parity rates.

When a change in the general price level occurred, therefore, this automatically resulted in the establishment of a new exchange parity, leading to a new external balance. This was unavoidable even though these parities were divorced from the former gold parity. Thus, the fluctuation in the exchange rates meant in fact a constant change of parity. If this balance could have been achieved easily, then, theoretically speaking, international currency reserves would have been unnecessary.

In fact, however, the changes in the value of the currency made it quite difficult to restore the external balance of payments, because a movement of funds that proved destructive to such a balance was encouraged, instead of an international movement of funds which, under the gold standard system, contributed to the restoration of such a balance. There were two reasons for this.

The first, already mentioned, was that under a fluctuating rate system interest earned could not be clearly calculated, and those purely speculative operations which merely took advantage of the fluctuations of exchange rates were considered more profitable.

[1] League of Nations, *International Currency Experience*, 1944, p. 143.

Secondly, the exchange reserves accumulated by most countries during the days of the gold exchange standard system provided a basis for the movement of funds.

Moreover, the insecurity of a currency gave rise to a flight of capital from that currency, leading to an intense international movement of so-called bad money or hot money, and this outflow was largely responsible for temporary violent changes in exchange rates, entirely divorced from the real parity. Further, the fluctuations in the exchange rates caused movements in the domestic level of commodity prices and gave a further impetus to speculation, thereby creating a vicious circle. This insecurity and instability brought about the following changes in the field of finance and exchange.

As already mentioned, the discount policy of a central bank became externally ineffective. For example, Britain kept its official bank rate at 2 per cent from 1932 to the outbreak of the Second World War, as a low rate of interest was considered necessary for domestic reasons and it was not necessary to take the external position into account.

Secondly, there was the influence exercised by the activities and development of a forward exchange market.

In 1923, when J. M. Keynes wrote *A Tract on Monetary Reform*, forward exchange transactions were not a common practice and caused little comment. He was thus able to say on this: 'The nature of forward dealing in exchange is not generally understood. The rates are seldom quoted in the newspapers. There are few financial topics of equal importance which have received so little discussion or publicity.' [1]

Later, however, with the ever-widening fluctuations of exchange rates and the continuing insecurity of currencies, the technique of forward exchange made great strides and a market for it developed. When exchange dealings increased greatly, as stated above, forward exchange was used to a great extent as a means of speculation.

International movements of funds taking advantage of a higher rate of interest are effected by means of a swap exchange operation. This gives rise to an interest parity and is seldom detrimental to the balance of payments. A speculative transaction, however, is mainly carried through by an outright

[1] J. M. Keynes, *A Tract on Monetary Reform*, p. 121.

forward exchange operation. Thus, bullish speculation in favour of the currency of a country with high interest rates would cause the foreign exchange market to be flooded with forward exchange purchases with the result that either the forward rate will rise, or its decline will be prevented, thereby obstructing or delaying the development of a true interest parity. In consequence, the inflow of funds through arbitrage transactions will increase. Should, however, speculation be bearish, the forward exchange rate would fall more rapidly and the gap become wider. Granting this to be so, it would seem that the speculative movement of funds in itself tends toward an equilibrium; but, in practice, speculative demand more often than not is apt to feed on itself and thus exert a detrimental influence on the balance of payments, and this in turn would prejudice the results of the application of a bank rate increased for the purpose of maintaining external equilibrium. This would be especially so in a bearish market as there is a point of equilibrium before the expected inflow of funds takes place and thus the effects of raising the bank rate are thereby partly nullified.

Even if there is no speculation, when exchange rates are allowed to fluctuate freely until the balance of payments becomes favourable, there is often the danger that the productive resources of a country would continually oscillate between the domestic and export markets. To permit such short-term fluctuations in exchange rates, bringing about such temporary changes, would in the long run be of little benefit.

In addition, under a system of floating exchange rates, it is impossible, even with the development of a forward exchange market, to cover the real exchange risk over an extended period, or influence the trend of exchange rates; and this obstructs a healthy international flow of funds and international trade.

For the purpose of removing this unhealthy situation, therefore, and of adjusting the conflict between the principle of national sovereignty concerning monetary policy, and the demands made of a member of the world monetary organization, it was proposed to create an exchange stabilization fund as a compromise between the above two principles.[1] Its

[1] League of Nations, *International Currency Experience*, 1944, p. 143.

objective was, internally, not only to guide the central bank in its policy regarding the international movement of gold (that is, to rely upon a discount policy), but also to carry out an adjustment of its credit solely by open market operations and, externally, to enable the authorities concerned to intervene in the exchange market when necessary and thereby prevent a wide deviation of the exchange rate from its parity. In other words, it was to provide a new device for the international control of gold.

As a result of going off the gold standard it is true that many countries prohibited the export of gold, but this did not mean that gold settlements between central banks were entirely eliminated.

In Britain, the obligation of the central bank to convert into gold was cancelled, but the export and import of gold was not prohibited, and the gold market in London remained in being till the eve of the Second World War. The United States operated a controlled currency system, but continued to export gold to gold standard countries and did not entirely do away with the external conversion into gold. France also maintained a gold standard system until 1936 but, even after that, only temporarily prohibited the export of gold, though it did suspend convertibility into gold. Thus, the controlled currency system was not then tied to an actual control of exchange. Therefore, it can be said that the world then was under practically the same world currency system as it is today.

This being so, from the standpoint of the international control of gold, a final controller always existed somewhere, and, if only each country adjusted its exchange with the currency of the controller, it would be able to retain the connection of its currency with gold.

Thus the gold market in London was controlled indirectly, just as it is today, and no violent fluctuations were permitted.

Settlements in gold were gradually effected not by actual shipments of gold, but by transfers between gold accounts, that is, by earmarking gold so that central banks, by economizing in shipping costs, could so much more freely adjust their exchange between the gold export and import points. In fact, this is the actual position in the so-called 'international gold settlement system'.

It was under such circumstances as are mentioned above, that the technique of the stabilization fund was used in order to control the currency externally. Its function was the difficult one of adjusting and maintaining a suitable level for the currency's external value while ensuring an appropriate level of domestic interest and commodity prices.

The fund was generally styled a stabilization fund, but its organization and objectives were different in the various countries concerned.

For example, the Exchange Equalization Account established in Britain in 1932 had as its objective the prevention of an abnormal rise in the exchange rate of the pound in response to an inflow of short-term funds, and also that of neutralizing the impact of the inflow on the domestic market. The reason why it was called an equalization account is that, at first, it did not actually possess any cash, but merely held treasury bills which were sold when necessity arose. Therefore, its resources were never fixed, but were constantly changing according to need. For example, if sterling had to be sold, the treasury bills were turned into cash, and the resulting funds were used to buy foreign currency or gold. If, however, for the purpose of the fund operations, foreign currency or gold had to be sold, the resulting sterling was used to buy treasury bills. The sale of treasury bills to the Bank of England allowed the inflow of foreign currency to influence the home market and tended to have an inflationary effect, but if treasury bills were sold to the market, the tendency was deflationary and thus neutralized the influence of the inflow of foreign currency. The skilful operation of the Fund achieved excellent results, owing to the well-organized financial and banking system in London.

The United States of America and some other countries launched their stabilization funds with gold assets from the very beginning, by providing them with those gold revaluation profits which had accompanied devaluation. Countries other than the United States found the above system more favourable than any other because their immediate concern was to prevent a decline in their exchange rates and maintain new parities. The United States of America, however, just like Britain, was in the position of having to resort to the selling of dollars and, therefore, was at first obliged to sell gold to the Federal Reserve

Bank to raise dollar funds. As, however, this operation was fraught with the danger of inflation at home, the system was later (in 1936) changed, in that the Treasury sold government bills to obtain dollar funds and kept the gold thus purchased in an 'inactive account', that is, it utilized the sterilization formula.

At this point, it may be necessary to explain the character of 'the stabilization fund system' in relation to the IMF system to be discussed later.

In the first place, 'the stabilization fund', though it was a measure for monetary control, was never free from the bondage of gold. Therefore, its operations on the exchange market were not quite free. It was, in essence, a mechanism for controlling the exchange, but its control was never very conclusive and it could not function beyond the amount of gold funds placed at its disposal. Thus 'stabilization funds' were 'instituted, not to replace but to supplement, the traditional system under which central banks and their treasuries bought and sold gold at a fixed price'.[1] In short, its character and functions were the negation of a floating exchange rate and recognized the transfer of reserves for the purpose of stabilizing an exchange rate.

Secondly, in the case of Britain, she insured herself against a short-term imbalance but retained a flexible and elastic policy for long-term adjustment of an imbalance.[2] These differing methods were introduced into the IMF organization, where security has been obtained by the principle of a fixed parity and elasticity has been secured by the possibility of changing it. There was, however, a serious obstruction to the operation of a stabilization fund at that time when looked at from an international angle.

As was stated above, though the rate on the London gold market was regulated indirectly by an international control of gold, yet that control, inevitably, gradually became weaker as the number of those countries which had given up the gold standard increased.

Thus, the foreign stabilization funds were unavoidably preoccupied with the gold value of the pound. That is, it was

---

[1] League of Nations, *International Currency Experience*, 1944, p. 145.
[2] R. F. Harrod, *The Pound Sterling*, as translated into Japanese under the title *Gendai-no-Pondo* and published by the Shiseido, p. 15.

doubtful whether the sterling currency in the funds would be converted into gold at the rate expected. The same may be said of the balance in foreign currencies possessed by Britain's Exchange Equalization Account. In short, it is essential for the operation of a stabilization fund that the gold value of the currencies of the countries concerned should be secured as much as possible, and that no alteration of an exchange parity should be made arbitrarily by any country, but with the co-operation of all concerned.

With this object in view, an attempt was made at the preparatory meeting of the London Economic Conference held in 1933 to obtain an agreement on exchange signed by the United States, Britain and France. The proposal suggested co-operation between their stabilization funds and the creation of a common exchange fund. Though this proposal came to nothing at the time, in 1936, when the franc was devalued, a currency agreement — the Tripartite Agreement — was signed by these three countries. Under this agreement, they guaranteed that their stabilization funds should be convertible into gold at the rates fixed for their holdings of those currencies. However, the values of gold were not fixed and, if the need arose in the economy of the country concerned, this commitment could be cancelled at 24 hours' notice. Thus the agreement was called a 24-Hours' Gold Standard, based on the contention that 24 hours were sufficient for the foreign currency holdings to be converted into gold. This agreement, therefore, gave priority to the domestic economy of a country, and was cynically labelled a 'companionate marriage and armed truce'. Nurkse says in his work often quoted here: 'As a general rule such exchange adjustments as may prove necessary after the establishment of an initial system should be made by mutual consultation and agreement. It ought to be an elementary principle of international monetary relations that exchange rates should not be altered by arbitrary unilateral action. The Tripartite Agreement was a belated and half-hearted admission of this principle.' [1]

However, each country had in setting up its currency limited the change of its gold parity to within 10 per cent of the old parity, and allowed scope for a further reduction of

[1] League of Nations, *International Currency Experience*, 1944, p. 141.

this limit. Later, Belgium, the Netherlands and Switzerland participated in this agreement, and there was thus an agreement for exchange stabilization among the six countries.

The principle of all countries getting together and guaranteeing their mutual parities should facilitate the stabilization of each other's exchange. This, after all, is the basic principle of the IMF system of which, in this sense, this agreement may be said to be the forerunner.

However, this international co-operation did not survive the great political upheaval of the Second World War (in 1939) and the drawbacks that were inherent in the stabilization fund system itself. One of the basic conditions for its success was the possession of abundant gold and foreign exchange. In the case of France, however, the outflow of short-term funds compelled her heavily to support the franc and thus rapidly to exhaust its stabilization fund, which had amounted to as much as 10 billion francs.

From the outset, the stabilization fund system was, as stated above, a compromise between two contradictory principles and, therefore, when these clashed, there was only one of two courses to follow: either to follow the line expected from a member of the international currency organization, which meant a return to the gold standard system, or to submit to the demands of the domestic economy, which is tantamount to negation of the principle of 'not resorting to exchange control' and 'aiming at exchange stabilization' embodied in the Tripartite Agreement. Thus, such countries as France often resorted to devaluation and, finding that measure insufficient, had recourse to exchange control on the outbreak of the war. Indeed, the war made such measures necessary with the result that during that conflict the exchange rate remained fixed while the stabilization fund, having lost its function, was utilized as an implement for the prosecution of the war.

MEANING AND PROBLEMS OF
FOREIGN EXCHANGE CONTROL

FOREIGN exchange control, which gradually gathered force after the panic of the 1930s, contained within itself a germ often disregarded by those concerned. It was that exchange control was in practice not only a method of adjusting the external position of a country but also that of its monetary organization.

The history of international monetary organization, which has been discussed in the preceding chapters, shows that this organization has gradually moved from natural control by gold to a form of artificial control. This tendency was accelerated by the direct control of exchange and trade, which was, in turn, an expression of the growing role played by the state in the national economy,[1] as for instance notably in Germany, Italy and Japan.

Looked at from another angle, the above tendency was a process of achieving that self-reliance in currency matters demanded by economic nationalism, to avoid a recurrence of deflation or a strengthening of armaments beyond the limit of resources, and exchange control was a means by which the authorities of such a country carried out its own monetary policy in its own independent interest without regard to external considerations. In this sense, it may be said that self-reliance in currency matters was successful to a certain extent. But in this success the application of exchange control resulted in the destruction of the international monetary organization. Indeed, it meant 'deliberately sacrificing some of the potential benefits of the international division of labour in return for fuller employment at home'.[2] Not only was this so, but its success was only of limited effect.

Thus, as a result of each country developing its self-reliant

---

[1] League of Nations, *International Currency Experience*, 1944, p. 186.
[2] *Ibid.*

domestic policy behind the protective wall of direct control, there emerged considerable discrepancies between domestic and international commodity price levels. As the policy of such countries was inevitably inflationary, aiming at eliminating depression and preparing for the war, the level of commodity prices at home was naturally higher than the international level.

If matters had been left as they were, the country concerned would have been swamped by a large inflow of imports. To counteract this, therefore, many countries resorted to subsidizing exports and to imposing duties or similar taxes on imports. Such a double price measure was in effect equivalent to a concealed devaluation or to a multiple exchange rate system.

The possibilities of such an adjustment policy were, however, somewhat limited. The arbitrary execution of domestic policies is fraught with the danger of a limitless reinforcement of external barriers and, finally, national isolation. This is the first disadvantage of exchange control.

Another is that it invites bilateralism in international trade and finance which, when it gets into its stride, requires a further strengthening of controls. The result is a vicious circle.

The reinforcement of exchange control results in the loss of currency convertibility, for, though under a free exchange international settlements are reflected in the accounts of foreign banks through multilateral exchange operations on the exchange market, the concentration of exchange operations causes the collapse of this free market, and, in consequence, resort has to be had to artificial financial and settlement systems as formed by many countries for international finance and settlements, necessitating inevitably the conclusion of various exchange and finance agreements. The same applies to bilateral trade which requires a bilateral system of finance and settlement. The overall result is the emergence of bilateralism, which is nothing but the principle of bilateral agreement; but, of whatever kind it may be, a bilateral agreement cannot avoid the question of final settlement.

Final settlement can be made only in gold or in a currency which is convertible into gold. Exchange control, therefore, did not aim at denying the importance of gold but only at its economy. While each country reinforced its exchange control, it made every effort to obtain gold or other similar settlement media.

Therefore, if a balance is not struck between two countries and measures for a settlement are not provided (as was the case with many international transactions), then they are forced to choose between two alternatives: to add to the shorter pole or cut a part off the longer one. Explaining this further, if one country is a debtor, it is often because it is short of those commodities which can be exported bilaterally, and, as a result, exports from the creditor country are reduced (*i.e.* the longer pole is cut short), the existing credit is cancelled unilaterally, or is frozen; that is, the debt is not met. The country that is placed in an unfavourable position is always the weaker of the two. Bilateralism was often used by the stronger to browbeat the weaker.

In order to break this impasse, recourse was had to a multilateral agreement, but as this covered only a small area, it could not give its fullest expression.

For the outside world, it was nothing but a 'multilateral bilateralism'; and those countries not in the agreement were liable to discriminatory treatment.

Why was this so? It was because bilateralism was often abused for political purposes, and its multilateral aspect only led to a closed circuit.

The third objection to exchange control is that, once it is set in motion, it inevitably leads to a more comprehensive form of control, because the external economic relations of a country may be so elaborate, and its markets so diffused over an area, that its laws and regulations cannot cover them all: as a result, it is technically very difficult to exercise efficient overall control.

In many cases, therefore, control, originally imposed to prevent the flight of capital, was gradually extended to cover current account transactions, thus suffocating the creative and mobile functions of commerce, and becoming inefficient thereby.

The fourth objection to exchange control is that the enforcement of control by one country is apt to lead to control by others.

If, for example, France's exchange control leads to the

franc being non-convertible, Britain is compelled to limit the convertibility of the non-resident sterling accounts held by France, because the funds thus accumulated are hard currency as a result of the use by France of sterling for its payments to the sterling area, and these now represent a threat to Britain's reserves.

Moreover, France, wishing to obtain sterling funds, will endeavour to increase her exports to Britain or to the British Commonwealth. Britain will be forced, therefore, to limit transfers to hard currency areas of those sterling balances held by a soft currency country such as France, and, in consequence, the convertibility of a non-resident sterling account will be impaired. On the other hand, the relaxation or abolition of control will be most effective if put into operation simultaneously by many countries.

It can therefore be seen that control has the effect of progressively reducing international economic transactions. Indeed, it should not be resorted to in normal times except in cases of monetary or political insecurity. (That control does restrict international relations in such emergencies was proved by the serious dollar shortage in the post-war period.)

In order to bring about the expansion of the world economy following the war, a start had to be made with the abolition of the control of trade and exchange and, especially, with the abolition of bilateralism.

The fifth evil created by exchange control is that it brings about a false balance.

As is well known, an international organization of exchange rates, if natural rate levels are permitted, should give rise to a horizontal, multilateral balance as a result of arbitrage transactions. Also between the spot and forward rates, a relative stability should arise through arbitrated interest rates. If, however, those exchange rates which ensure reciprocal payments between two countries are fixed artificially, the organic relation between those rates is lost, with the result that the organization of exchange rates will not represent a true picture of the effective value of the various cross rates. The vertical relations between the spot and forward exchange rates are no exception to this. Such artificial fixing of rates, though a hindrance, was not a complete bar to international commercial relations.[1]   The trouble, however, was that it continued to distort the rational flow of funds and commodities between countries, but little notice was taken at the time of such a deplorable state of affairs.   It can be stated that the economic loss suffered by the world in general due to such a situation was unaccountably great.   Therefore, one of the objectives of international economic plans during the post-war years was the reconstruction of the lost rational international relations as soon as possible.

[1] League of Nations, *International Currency Experience*, 1944, p. 182.

V

BIRTH OF THE
BRETTON WOODS AGREEMENTS

Section 1.—The American Point of View

ONE of the factors that contributed to the great change in the world economy after the Second World War was the change of the United States of America's attitude towards it.

As is well known, the United States had a long tradition of isolationism which was of little help to the world economy.

When faced with a situation it did not like, the United States always withdrew into its isolationist shell, a retreat made possible by the self-sufficiency of its economy. It is not too much to say that the United States then had comparatively little experience of participation in the organization of the world economy.

As a result of the two world wars the United States became the greatest of all creditor nations, and such isolationism became out-dated and untenable. With the passing of time the United States came to acquire the confidence that it could stand up to international competition on an equal footing and, moreover, became conscious of its duty and ability to take a leading position in the world economy, as and when this was thought desirable.

In this complete change of course, the United States was faced with two obstacles, one being the direct control of trade and the other the instability of exchange rates.

The reason was that the aim of exchange control and discrimination through bilateralism was to economize on hard currencies, and this adversely affected the countries with such currencies. The greatest victim was the U.S. dollar, which was a hard currency.

More particularly, the greatest concern of the United States and its greatest threat was the sterling area currency bloc.

The sterling area was a currency bloc which developed about the time of the collapse of the gold standard system after the First World War. It gradually became an elaborate system and from sheer necessity was tightened during the Second World War. However, the United States, with her new self-confidence in international competition, was in a position to overcome this obstacle by promoting multilateral transactions based upon freedom and equality.

Of the two elements of control, restriction and discrimination, the latter was of greater concern to the United States, and its aim, therefore, was to persuade all nations to abolish their discriminatory measures. In other words, it had, first of all, to do away with bilateralism. Thus, the fundamental principle upheld by the United States for the working of world economy following the war, was that of multilateralism.

More than anything else, the United States required stable exchange rates in order to secure widespread acceptance of its own policies as the leader in the world economy. But even if the United States had been successful in abolishing bilateralism and exchange control, it would not have been able to permeate the domestic economy of other countries with its own policies, so long as they could arbitrarily alter their exchange rates to suit their own convenience. That all should maintain absolutely stable exchange rates (including the gold parity of U.S. dollar) and should forgo the urge to devalue, became for the United States of paramount importance for the application of its principles of post-war exchange methods.

On the other hand, Britain, which had for a long time held the leadership in world economy, owing to the nature of its economy, required an increase in world trade and in international co-operation as the indispensable foundation of its prosperity. Britain, therefore, had no reason to oppose multilateral transactions on a free and non-discriminatory basis, principles enshrined in its traditional liberalism in trade; but the fact remained that Britain had lost very considerable external assets and gold reserves in the two world wars. Moreover, as a result of the difference in productivity between the two countries, Britain had lost confidence in its ability to compete internationally on an equal footing with the United States. Furthermore, it had to face the grave immediate problem of how to raise the enormous sums required for its economic reconstruction, and the longer run problem of how to secure equilibrium in its balance of payments. These, and how it should reconstruct its domestic economy and achieve full employment without taking into account its external economic relations, were the most urgent problems for Britain at the time. It was not, however, to be expected that Britain would thus early dismantle its trade and exchange restrictions and relinquish bilateralism. If it did, how could it reconcile its contradictory requirements? This certainly was a very difficult question.

Now it can be seen why the United States and Britain, though from different angles and for different reasons, began to give consideration to those problems which were concerned with the post-war economy under the common necessity of international co-operation. What followed was the Bretton Woods Agreements. This was in effect a compromise between the two schools of thought. It will be an advantage to discuss fully the views held by the two countries, and to trace the course of the negotiations that preceded the Agreements, since this will help us to understand its nature, and will at the same time prepare us for a re-examination of the world monetary organization, which is now being discussed so fully.

Let us, then, first of all consider the point of view of the United States of America.

The great principles of post-war reorganization were already being studied in the United States on a broad scale by the leading departments of the Administration. According to Gardner, there were three main planning sections: first, the State Department headed by the Secretary of State, Cordell Hull, and the Under-Secretary of State, Sumner Welles; second, the Treasury Department with Secretary of the Treasury, Henry Morgenthau, and Assistant Secretary of the Treasury, Harry Dexter White, who was in charge of international finance; and third, a group centred round Vice-President Henry A. Wallace of the Board of Economic Warfare.[1]

These planners, whose respective views had somewhat different nuances, were determined, from the lessons learnt after the First World War, not to commit the same errors again.

[1] Richard N. Gardner, *Sterling-Dollar Diplomacy*, 1956, p. 4.

These errors were (1) that the United States had not joined the League of Nations, and had taken an indifferent attitude toward the post-war world economy and (2) that, being pre-occupied with political questions, they had neglected economic matters.

Incidentally, the above-mentioned officials, excepting Hull, were survivors of the so-called New Dealers, and were almost united in regarding as important the role to be played by the state in the economy. In particular, they had no confidence in the capacity of private Wall Street financiers in the field of finance. Morgenthau, for example, is said to have defined the objective of post-war plans as 'moving the financial centre of the world from London and Wall Street to the United States Treasury; and to create a new concept between nations in international finance'. The main objective of the planners in the Treasury Department, therefore, was believed to have been not so much to rehabilitate the sector of private enter-prise as to create such an expansion on a global basis as would be in conformity with the New Deal's social and economic objectives.[1]

It is said that the post-war plans of the United States were formulated as early as the autumn of 1939 by Dr. Leo Pasvolsky, then special adviser to the Secretary of the Treasury,[2] and that this elaborate memorandum was taken across the Atlantic and shown to J. M. Keynes, who at the time was also formulating a plan from the British point of view. Indeed, it is thought to have been the first blueprint of the Bretton Woods Agreements. According to Harrod's *The Life of John Maynard Keynes*, Keynes is said to have reacted as follows to the above memorandum:

'Somewhat later a stimulus of a different kind came across the waters, in the form of a very able memorandum by Mr. Pasvolsky, which pointed out how fatal it would be for Britain to abandon her traditional open trade. Keynes was critical of it; he deemed Mr. Pasvolsky a Rip van Winkle, who knew nought of the stresses and strains to which trade had been subjected in the 'thirties or modern diagnoses of those maladies; none the less, he admitted that the document was convincing within the limits of its own thinking and

---

[1] Richard N. Gardner, *Sterling-Dollar Diplomacy*, 1956, p. 76.
[2] *Ibid.* p. 72.

should be taken seriously as evidence of the American point of view.'[1]

At this point, it may be necessary to discuss 'multilateralism', which was the central theme of the post-war programme of the United States.

The reason why the United States favoured the multilateral system was that it desired in theory the elimination of economic nationalism and economic isolationism, which were the result of pre-war and war-time circumstances, but in practice wished particularly to do away with the preferential tariff system of the British Commonwealth, which had been a bad feature of its international commercial relations; and, at the same time, it sought to persuade all nations, including those of the British Commonwealth, to reduce to the greatest possible extent their direct control of trade and foreign exchanges.

But it should be noted that the relaxation of direct control did not necessarily mean the free trade of former days, for the chief aim of the United States was to eliminate discrimination; therefore, the relaxation of general control was but a secondary objective and, moreover, the United States, which had adopted protection itself, was in no position to urge strongly upon others the abolition of obstacles to trade in general.

Thus, even in the field of finance, the demands of the United States might not necessarily have been for the restoration of convertibility internally, but, rather, the restoration of the convertibility of non-resident accounts, which was of more importance to the United States than that of resident accounts which was only a secondary consideration.[2]

A definition of multilateralism may be said to be found in the Atlantic Charter, published in August 1941. It seems that various schemes were proposed by the United States and Britain from their respective viewpoints, but that the term came to

[1] R. F. Harrod, *The Life of John Maynard Keynes*, 1951, p. 528.

It is said that prior to this, Alvin Hansen and L. H. Gulick, consultant of the National Planning Board, visited Britain, and advocated co-operation between the United States and Britain, by proposing the formation of an International Economic Board as an advisory organ for the participating countries on domestic policies designed to promote full employment, economic stabilization and world trade, and also on researches into international resources and into the setting up of an international Development Bank for economic development. (Harrod, *ibid.* pp. 527-8.)

[2] R. N. Gardner, *ibid.* p. 13.

mean in effect that the two nations, taking into account their
existing obligations, should bend their efforts to enable all
nations, great or small, victorious or vanquished, to benefit
under equal conditions from these material resources of the
world which were necessary for their trade and economic
prosperity. (Article 4 of the Charter.) Article 5 also lays
down that the two countries hope that all nations would co-
operate in all economic sectors so that the two might be able
to ensure improved labour standards, economic development
and social security.[1] These requirements were considered
important as means towards achieving President Roosevelt's
so-called 'freedom from poverty'.

This definition of multilateralism was confirmed in Article 7
of the Mutual Aid Agreement signed in February 1942. This
was regarded as the legal framework for post-war economic
programmes, according to which,

(1) each nation could participate in the post-war co-operation
of the United States and Britain on the following conditions:
(2) it intended expanding, through suitable international and
domestic measures, production, employment, exchange,
and consumption of goods, which measures constituted the
basis of liberty and the welfare of all peoples;
(3) it has the intention of removing every form of discrimination and of reducing tariffs and other barriers to international trade, that is, it has the intention of achieving
those economic objectives which are contained in the
Joint Declaration (meaning the Atlantic Charter) of the
United States and Britain.[2]

How, then, could the common intentions of the two
countries be realized in concrete form? To provide the
answer to this, the two countries referred the matter to their
experts, requesting them to formulate plans for currency and
finance. In America, it was the Treasury Department, with

[1] Richard N. Gardner, *Sterling-Dollar Diplomacy*, 1956, pp. 46-7.
Though the actual definition of the 'existing obligations' mentioned therein
is not clear, Britain perhaps meant by this expression its vested interests, such as
its preferential system.
[2] R. N. Gardner, *ibid.* pp. 58-9.

Harry D. White as the principal official involved, that was given this task.

In *The Life of John Maynard Keynes*, Harrod says of White: 'In Britain, he is too often thought of as some dim scribe, some kind of robot, who wrote at the behest of that vaguely conceived entity, the American Treasury, an inferior version of the Keynes Plan — mainly to vex the British! Far different was the real man. He was a very remarkable figure, who should be accorded an honourable place in British annals.' [1]

According to the same source, he was educated at Harvard and studied under Viner. When Secretary of the Treasury Morgenthau entrusted Viner with the study of fiscal and financial matters, White also participated, thus gradually winning the confidence of the Secretary of the Treasury and occupying an influential position in his department. He also took part in the conclusion of the Tripartite Agreement and in the operations of the American Exchange Stabilization Fund. During the First World War he had been a leading figure in the Treasury. He was, therefore, in practice, an authority on United States international financial matters. He is said to have been an ardent admirer of Keynes so far as his academic views are concerned.[2]

It was therefore not strange that White should have been chosen as the chief planner on the American side. In 1938–1939, he had been working on the idea of an Inter-American Bank. Though this plan came to nothing owing to opposition from some quarters, he had, about the end of 1941, evolved an outline of the so-called White Plan. In December of that year, Morgenthau entrusted him with the working out of a Treasury plan dealing with post-war financial policies. The blueprint of this plan was informally presented to the authorities concerned under the title of 'Suggested Plan for a United Nations Stabilization Fund and Bank for Reconstruction of the United and Associated Nations'. (It was, however, not made public.)

[1] R. F. Harrod, *The Life of John Maynard Keynes*, 1951, pp. 537-8.
[2] *Ibid.* p. 538.

Section 2.—The White Plan

Prior to this, there had existed in the United States the Feis Plan (a trade stabilization fund and budget) published in January 1942 by Herbert Feis, economic adviser to the State Department.

According to this plan, the United States should establish a credit in favour of sundry foreign countries amounting to $3 to $4 billion, the minimum annual amount, to enable them to meet their payments to the United States. These countries were to fix their share by negotiation and, at the same time, open an account in the name of the United States in their respective currencies or in third party currencies to the equivalent value of the amount already utilized, at an agreed rate of exchange. The balance standing to the credit of the United States in the currency of the country concerned when utilized would be reduced by the cost of such purchases or services at the equivalent dollar rate. Finally, the balance of the two accounts, when not utilized, would be cancelled after a certain lapse of time.[1]

The White Plan itself underwent various vicissitudes before it was made public. The project was altered twice, so that there were three versions. According to Gardner, besides the original version there were two others typewritten and mimeographed in March and April 1942, respectively. Though the second and third were not very different from one another, the first differed markedly from the final draft.[2]

The original plan was very ambitious, having the character of a financial department of, as it were, a world government. It stipulated that the stabilization fund should hold funds of $5 billion consisting of gold currencies and government securities of the participating countries, to meet their demand for short-term loans to overcome difficulties in their balance of payments. The fund was also given the power of limiting very considerably the economic sovereignty of each participating country by unilaterally changing its exchange rate, abolishing exchange control, and supervising its domestic economic

---

[1] These provisions were later given material expression to some extent in the counterpart funds of various countries that accompanied American aid or drawing rights.   [2] Richard N. Gardner, *Sterling-Dollar Diplomacy*, 1956, p. 74.

policies. The fund was, therefore, largely of an international character and had some pretensions to being an element in a planned economy.

The 'bank' of the plan was much more ambitious than the fund, its capital (joint stock) amounting to as much as $10 billion, half to be paid immediately. (In the existing World Bank system only 20 per cent of its capital is for immediate payment.)

The 'bank's' funds were to be used not merely for financing economic reconstruction and the development of undertakings, but also, if necessary, for making contracyclical investments at a time of world depression. (In the existing IMF and World Bank this function is entirely absent.)

Moreover, the bank was authorized to purchase and to sell gold and negotiable securities of the member countries, and to discount and re-discount bills (including bank acceptances).

These two international financial organizations, therefore, were constituted in such a way as to be capable of taking a large part in the activities of all fields of international finance, both in the post-war transition and in more normal times.

In the spring of 1942 two inter-departmental committees were constituted in the United States of America, one consisting of the secretaries of the various departments and the other of the technical experts of those departments. (In the Technical Committee, members of the Board of the Federal Reserve System and the Security Exchange Commission also participated.) As a result of their deliberations, the broad scope of the plan detailed above was gradually whittled away; and, as the stabilization fund plan was given priority, the Treasury Department group headed by White, being on the defensive, saw its proposals gradually take second place. Further, in the Congressional elections of that year, the Democratic Party lost many seats and the conservatives in the Republican Party began to exercise political pressure. Thus, the initial ideas entertained by White suffered important amendments, so that the amended plan made public in April 1943 contained nothing about the 'bank', and took account of susceptibilities regarding national sovereignty in respect of the stabilization fund. As compared with the original, the amended plan showed marked signs of a return to nationalism.

This White Plan (styled a Preliminary Draft Outline of Protocol for an International Stabilization Fund of the United and Associated Nations) was further amended in July 1943 and was further discussed by experts from thirty nations. Finally, it became the prototype of the International Monetary Fund (IMF). If we examine its details, however, it is clear that it was of a far more international character than the IMF. Its main principles are as follows:

In its preamble, the plan asserts that:

1. Progress toward the establishment of a functioning democratic world in the post-war period will depend on the ability of free peoples to work together in solving their economic problems. Not the least of these is the problem of how to prevent a widespread breakdown of currencies with resultant international economic disorder.
2. The free countries will not resort to competitive exchange depreciation, multiple currency practices, discriminatory bilateral clearing or other destructive foreign exchange devices.
3. These are not transitory problems of the immediate post-war period affecting only a few countries.
4. The International Stabilization Fund of the United and Associated Nations is proposed as a permanent institution for international monetary co-operation.
5. The Fund would deal only with member governments and their fiscal agents, and would not intrude on the customary channels for conducting international commerce and finance.

The purposes include (*a*) to help stabilize foreign exchange rates, (*b*) to shorten the periods and lessen the degree of disequilibrium in the international balance of payments, (*c*) to help create conditions under which the smooth flow of foreign trade and of productive capital would be fostered, (*d*) to facilitate the effective utilization of blocked foreign balances and (*e*) to reduce the use of foreign exchange restrictions and other discriminatory practices. Therefore the following provisions are proposed:

1. The Fund should have resources of not less than $5 billion.
2. The member countries are required to make payment of part of their quotas (minimum 30 per cent) in gold, the

balance being payable in their own currency with an option that payment of up to 50 per cent of their quotas may be made in government securities. The member countries may include in their legal reserves the amount of their contributions in gold less their net purchases of foreign exchange from the Fund paid for with local currencies.

3. The quota for each member shall be calculated on the basis of its foreign exchange reserves, balance of payments, national income, etc. Quotas shall be adjusted on the basis of the most recent data three years after the establishment of the Fund, and at intervals of five years thereafter.

4. The monetary unit of the Fund shall be the Unitas, equal in value to $137\frac{1}{7}$ grains of fine gold (equivalent to $10). No change in the gold value of the Unitas shall be made except with the approval of 85 per cent of the member votes.

5. The value of the currency of each member country shall be established in terms of Unitas. No member country shall deal in gold, directly or indirectly, at a price in terms of its national currency in excess of, or below the parity (which corresponds to the value of its currency in terms of Unitas and to the value of Unitas in terms of gold).

6. Changes in the exchange value of the currency of a member country shall be considered only when essential for the correction of a fundamental disequilibrium in its balance of payments, and shall be made only with the approval of three fourths of the member votes, including the representative of the country concerned.

Because of the extreme uncertainties of the immediate post-war period, the following exceptional provisions may be in force during the first three years of the Fund's operations :

(a) When the existing rate of exchange of a member country is clearly inconsistent with the maintenance of a balanced international payments position for that country, changes from the established rate may be made at the special request of that country and with the approval of a majority of the member votes.

(b) A member country may change the established rate for its currency by not more than 10 per cent provided that the member country shall notify the Fund of its intention and shall consult with the Fund on the advisability of its action.

7. The Fund shall determine the range within which the rates of exchange of member currencies shall be permitted to fluctuate.

8. The Fund shall have the power to buy, sell and hold gold, currencies and government securities of member countries; to earmark and transfer gold; to issue its own debentures, and to offer them for discount or sale in member countries.

   The Fund shall purchase for local currency any foreign exchange acquired by a member of good standing from another member country in settlement of a balance of payments current account, where such currency cannot be disposed of in the foreign exchange markets within the range established by the Fund.

9. The Fund may sell under certain conditions to the treasury of any member country (or stabilization fund or central bank acting as its agent) at the accepted rate of exchange, currency of any member country held by the Fund.

10. When the currency of a member country is judged to be scarce (that is, when it becomes a so-called scarce currency) the Fund shall take measures to increase it and achieve a balance between supply and demand.

11. In order to promote the most effective use of the available and accumulating supply of foreign exchange resources of member countries, each member country agrees that it will offer to sell to the Fund, for its local currency or for foreign currencies which the member country needs, one-half of the foreign exchange resources and gold it acquires in excess of its official holdings at the time it became a member of the Fund.

    The Fund shall inform any member country when, in its opinion, any further growth of privately held foreign exchange and gold appears to be unwarranted.

    When the Fund's holdings of the local currency and securities of a member country exceed the quota of that country, the Fund shall, upon the request of the member country, resell to the member country the Fund's excess holdings of the currency of that country for gold or acceptable foreign exchange.

When the gold and free foreign exchange holdings of a member country exceed 50 per cent of its quota, the Fund (in selling foreign exchange to the member concerned) shall require that one-half of such exchange shall be paid in gold or foreign exchange acceptable to the Fund.

12. Each member undertakes:

To abandon, as soon as a member country decides that conditions permit, all restrictions (other than those involving capital transfers) regarding foreign exchange transactions with other member countries, and not to impose any additional restrictions (except upon capital transfers) without the approval of the Fund.

To co-operate effectively with other member countries when such countries, with the approval of the Fund, adopt or continue controls for the purpose of regulating international movements of capital.

13. Not to enter upon any new bilateral clearing arrangements, nor engage in multiple currency practices, which in the judgment of the Fund would retard the growth of world trade or the international flow of productive capital.

The foregoing cover the main principles of the so-called White Plan. Its original version was called a 'preliminary draft', and it was indeed nothing but a draft, without any definite form. Its meaning and contents, therefore, are not as clear as might be desirable and, moreover, there are no notes anywhere. Mrs. Robinson summed it up by saying 'It has to be read in the spirit of a detective story'.[1]

Therefore, it is rash to judge it only by its main principles; it is not easy to understand its true meaning unless we consider it in conjunction with the Keynes Plan to be discussed later. It may not be out of order, however, to comment on it briefly at this stage.

First, gold payments represent a very large percentage of the quota, and it is especially noteworthy that those payments are computed on the basis of reserves, balance of payments or national income of a member country. The large percentage of gold payments was no doubt designed to reinforce the

[1] Joan Robinson, 'The International Currency Proposals' (S. E. Harris, *The New Economics*, p. 349).

position of the fund and increase its authority, but the basis of computation is open to question. The United States of America, under such conditions, would naturally be granted the largest quota, and, in consequence, exercise the greatest voting power. Technically, it is very difficult to estimate correctly the precise value of the gold and foreign currency reserves and national income of a country. Under the then prevailing circumstances, however, it was only to be expected that the United States would become the greatest creditor country, and therefore it would be true to say that the efficiency of the activities of the Fund would depend upon its dollar holdings, and, in consequence, the granting of as great a quota as possible to the United States was of fundamental importance.[1]

Second, that a member country could count part of its subscription as belonging to its legal reserves, is worthy of notice from the point of view of international liquidity. It is interesting that Thomas Balogh recently proposed a similar plan for the reform of the IMF,[2] details of which will be given later.

Third, it is important that the quotas of member countries should be re-examined and readjusted periodically as circumstances change — (this point has been provided for in the IMF Agreement).

Fourth, a new unit of currency has been established, which, however, was intended merely as a unit for computation and was not designed to become a new international currency. 'The Unitas plan provides no international currency. Unitas is simply a word meaning gold to the value of $10 at the present price.'[3]

It should be noted, however, that the values of the member currencies are attached to gold through their representation by Unitas.

Further, it was the duty of all members to maintain the value in Unitas, that is, the gold value of each currency. Though there were no regulations for dealing with the domestic currency

[1] Joan Robinson, 'The International Currency Proposals' (S. E. Harris, *The New Economics*, p. 345).
[2] Thomas Balogh, 'International Reserves and Liquidity', *The Economic Journal*, June 1960. [3] Joan Robinson, *ibid.* p. 344.

system for every member, the Fund, as an international monetary organization, bore the character of a gold standard system, as is the current IMF organization.

However, the Fund does not control gold, which is the responsibility of the United States, so that the gold value of Unitas is in effect the value of the dollar. Thus, the Unitas is the U.S. dollar. Such being the case, this system is a dollar exchange standard system, as is the IMF Agreement.

Fifth, the White Plan had very rigidly fixed the selling and buying prices of gold for minting, and had adopted more rigid regulations than the IMF in matters concerning a change of parity. This marks it as a plan of American inspiration, as that country makes a fetish of the immutability of parities and the absolute maintenance of exchange rates.

Sixth, the Fund had authority to ear-mark and transfer gold, thus taking on a function which was formerly that of the Bank for International Settlements. Should it not be possible for the currencies of member countries to be exchanged at their official rates, the Fund is authorized to buy them and thus helps in maintaining the rates agreed upon. This gave the Fund a function of international settlement to a considerable degree, which, it is to be deplored, is absent from the current IMF system. The Fund can thus truly be called a 'Stabilization Fund'.

Seventh, provisions for the stabilization of balances of payments merit attention. The clause on a so-called scarce currency has been included in the IMF Agreement, which, in comparison, seems to lack the authority for imposing equilibrium even upon creditor countries.

Originally these provisions were a codification of the characteristics of the gold standard system, since the movement of gold automatically compelled both creditor and debtor nations to make every effort to adjust their balance of payments, and this is also recognized in the Keynes Plan to be touched upon later. Mrs. Robinson considered this point as being more unfavourable than the Keynes Plan to a creditor country.

It follows that those measures taken at a time of disequilibrium, tend to reduce the flow of exports from creditor nations and subject them immediately to deflationary pressure, but the Keynes Plan appears to leave some room for putting other measures into practice,[1] a point that will be discussed later. Mrs. Robinson adds, however, that such an interpretation of the plan may prove to be a misunderstanding which, none the less, may not necessarily be so. The practical point, however, is in what manner these provisions will be applied. There are no rules laid down as to how advice to a debtor country is to be given by the Fund (as to this the IMF has no power to do so). Thus these provisions, subject to the manner of their application, may reasonably be expected to put substantial pressure upon a creditor country.

Section 3.—The British Point of View

The American views and aspirations outlined in section 2 provide a setting for comparison with British beliefs and objectives.

The expectation, that in post-war days Britain would follow a line of international co-operation, can be traced to the following three factors.

First, it was known that Britain would find it necessary to have recourse to American aid, not only for the prosecution of the war but also for post-war reconstruction.

Second, there was the traditional regard for free trade in Britain, though it should be noted that Britain did not rate discrimination of great importance in the elimination of obstacles to trade. Here Britain tended to hold a view contrary to that prevailing in the United States.

Third, Britain had a strong desire for international collaboration in the political field. The Labour Party was particularly enthusiastic about establishing an international organization, through which international, political and economic problems could be ironed out on a planned basis.

In Britain, as in the United States, it was those economic experts who had been attached provisionally to various Ministries to meet the demand for war-time economic planning who were most prominent in discussing such planning. Among

---

[1] Joan Robinson, 'The International Currency Proposals' (S. E. Harris, *The New Economics*, pp. 348-9).

them were such leading economists as Lionel Robbins and James Meade. The views held by these men conformed to an orthodox free economy. In the Treasury there were such men as D. Robertson and J. M. Keynes, who also had no objection to multilateralism.

Outside government circles, however, there was general disbelief in multilateralism. Industrialists who had lost their trust in free competition, the traditionally anti-free trade agricultural interests and those in the Labour Party who supported a planned and controlled economy belonged to this group, which insisted that bilateralism was not to be lightly relinquished, and that the preferential duties of the British Commonwealth should be strictly adhered to.

Keynes and his plans stood between these two extreme opposing views. From a historical standpoint, his views may be regarded as a natural compromise.

Here let us take a look at Keynes's proposals. It is true that he had stigmatized the gold standard system as a 'barbarous relic'[1] and had for long been against it. His main reason for doing so was that the amount of international currency is 'determined in an unpredictable and irrelevant manner as, for example, by the technical progress of the gold industry'[2] and that 'any system is intolerable that necessitates, as a part of its normal and regular working, the artificial creation of unemployment from time to time'.[3]

When R. G. Hawtrey proposed in 1923 that Britain should return to the gold standard in co-operation with the United States, Keynes opposed it, arguing that, in a situation in which gold would be concentrated in the United States, the establishment of the gold standard system would mean entrusting the adjustment of commodity prices and the determination of economic cycles to the American Federal Reserve System.[4]

It is a mistake, however, to think that Keynes, while overemphasizing economic nationalism, intended to do away entirely with internationalism, or to infer that in pointing out the drawbacks of the gold standard, he wished wholly

---

[1] J. M. Keynes, *A Tract on Monetary Reform*, 1923, p. 172.
[2] R. F. Harrod, *The Life of John Maynard Keynes*, p. 526.
[3] R. F. Harrod, *Policy Against Inflation*, p. 30.
[4] J. M. Keynes, *ibid.* pp. 174-5.

E

to eliminate gold from the field of currency.

On the contrary, he opposed the view, held generally, that the war-time principle of control should be continued unchanged, and showed his dislike of returning to the 'principles of the jungle'. His instincts were for international co-operation, and it was because such co-operation then seemed impossible that they remained dormant for some years before the war.[1] If international co-operation had been advocated under pre-war conditions without restriction, there would have been a danger of a return to the international gold standard system. He saw it as a problem calling for measures to achieve international co-operation without returning to the gold standard system.

In a letter to *The Economist*, he wrote: 'At all stages of the post-war developments the credit proposals which I have brought forward from time to time, have been based on the *use of gold as an international standard* (the author's italics), while discarding it as a rigid national standard'.[2]

This was a passage in his defence against the criticism in 1945 that he was lacking in consistency in that he advocated an amended gold standard (that is, a gold standard enlarging the difference between the gold points and permitting an occasional change of gold parity). What he proposed in *A Tract on Monetary Reform* was to concentrate gold in the hands of a central bank and, by using it as an external buffer, provide a means of rectifying a short-term imbalance. He thought that if the United States established a wise control of gold, did not try to tie the value of the dollar to gold, ceased attempting foolishly to make the value of gold follow that of the dollar at considerable expense to themselves, aimed at the stabilization of the dollar against commodities rather than against gold, and pursued a policy of allowing the value of the dollar to fluctuate against gold, thereby stabilizing its value against commodities and thus co-operating with Britain, then the stabilization of exchange between the United States and Britain could be achieved almost immediately.

His ideas at the time regarding a world currency system were that countries other than the United States and Britain

[1] R. F. Harrod, *The Life of John Maynard Keynes*, pp. 525-6.
[2] *Ibid.* p. 445.

should not adopt an independent standard system, should be linked with either the pound or the dollar through the exchange standard system, hold domestic gold reserves against short-term fluctuations, and, by keeping balances in London and New York, achieve stability of exchange rates through manipulation of the Bank Rate and other means.[1]

The strong impression gained, following the war, that Keynes was more inclined toward internationalism, was partly due to the fact that he judged there was now no danger of international co-operation leading to a revival of the gold standard system. The apprehension felt at that time by the British in general, including Keynes, was that, as happened during the period between the two wars, a depression or the institution of deflationary policies in a creditor nation such as the United States, would spread to other countries, and thus involve Britain.

How, then, could such a trend be halted without resorting to bilateralism or control? The first step would be to allow the nations to alter their exchange rates or parities and give them a free hand in expansion, and the second, to devise such an organization as would compel even a creditor nation to go in for expansion following on an inflow of gold.

The revival of international co-operation in Keynes's view, therefore, was conditioned by the following:

First, the parity between a domestic currency and gold should not be rigid.

Second, the difference between the gold points should be widened.

And third, some kind of international control, if possible, should be enforced to adjust the commodity value of gold within certain limits.[2]

It is as well to recall that Keynes, in the 1930s, had already set out in *A Treatise on Money* the measures to be taken to resolve the contradictions between the internal and external aspects of currency control.

He emphasized the function of interest parity in the functions of exchange rates and in the difference among the interest rates of the various countries. As was pointed out in

---

[1] J. M. Keynes, *A Tract on Monetary Reform*, 1923, pp. 197-205.
[2] R. F. Harrod, *ibid.* p. 445.

Chapter III, Section 3, Keynes, aware that the greater the fluctuations in the exchange rates, that is, the greater the distance between the gold points, the smaller would be the attraction for foreign funds for any difference in interest rates,[1] proposed that the central bank's selling and buying prices for gold should be limited to around 2 per cent and that the weapon of the bank rate should be used by the central bank simultaneously with intervention in the forward exchange market.[2]

These measures, however, were only to be construed as a formula for the voluntary control of currency.

Keynes had already given expression to this idea in *A Tract on Monetary Reform*, in which he proposed that the Bank of England should adjust the value of gold as it did the discount rate, that is, the Bank of England should publish the gold selling and buying prices every Thursday morning together with its official discount rates, and also each day its three-month forward exchange rates. The only difference between this and his other proposal is that, in his former tract, he regarded gold only as an external reserve and emphasized that this was the only use for gold.[3] He thought that a combination of these British and American formulas for the control of gold and the maintenance of co-operation between the two countries would be sufficient to stabilize the British-American cross rate and the rates of other countries which were linked with them.

His argument was that the stability of the pound should never be sacrificed for the purpose of stabilizing the sterling-dollar rate.

For Britain, the internal stabilization of the pound should be the prime objective, but co-operation with the United States, 'aiming at exchange stability also as a secondary objective', would not be ruled out.[4] And 'it is the greatest advantage of the gold standard that it overcomes the excessive sensitiveness of the exchanges to temporary influences. Our objective must be to secure this advantage, if we can, without committing ourselves to follow big movements in the value of gold itself.'[5]

---

[1] J. M. Keynes, *A Treatise on Money*, 1930, p. 320.   [2] *Ibid.* pp. 325-31.
[3] J. M. Keynes, *A Tract on Monetary Reform*, pp. 190-5.
[4] *Ibid.* p. 183.   [5] *Ibid.* p. 189.

His arguments in his new treatise are not much different from those in his old tract on this point. If, he says, the above-mentioned formula for the voluntary control of currency can be guaranteed, it may be possible to recognize gold as standard international currency and make use of its great advantages. He explained this by saying that gold should be brought down from its tyrant's throne and converted into a constitutional sovereign, subject to the will of a cabinet consisting of all the central banks. Going further in his new treatise, he thought of carrying out the reform of gold control through the institution of a supranational organization,[1] and finally entertained the idea of a supranational bank (SNB).

Such an organization could not be set up at one stroke, but had to come about gradually. The main principles governing this system were as follows:

1. First, a conference of central banks should agree to the following rules for active co-operation:

    (*a*) Each country should refrain from putting gold into circulation, and only hold it as a reserve in its central bank.

    (*b*) Each country should also hold some foreign currency as a reserve.

    (*c*) The legal reserve requirements should be occasionally permitted to fluctuate within a margin of 20 per cent at the recommendation of the central banks' committee.

    (*d*) There should be a margin of 2 per cent between the minimum buying price and the maximum selling price of gold held by the central bank.

2. Then, going a step further, a supranational bank (SNB) should be established, and all central banks should have the same business relations with it as exist between a central bank and its domestic commercial banks. The essential characteristics of such a supranational bank, would be as follows:

    (*a*) SNB need not have an initial capital, but its liabilities should be guaranteed by all the central banks adhering to the scheme.

    (*b*) SNB should only have business relations with the central banks. Its assets should consist of gold, securities and

---

[1] J. M. Keynes, *A Treatise on Money*, p. 388.

advances to central banks, and its liabilities, of deposits by central banks. Such deposits should be called Supranational Bank-money (SBM).

(*c*) SBM should be bought for gold and sold for gold at fixed prices differing from one another by 2 per cent.

(*d*) SNB should independently fix the amount of its own gold reserves with no fixed rates against its liabilities.

(*e*) The national moneys of all the central banks adhering to the supranational bank should be compulsorily bought and sold in terms of SBM on the same terms as gold, *i.e.* with a difference of 2 per cent between the buying and the selling price. Furthermore, it would be very desirable that national moneys should only be exchanged for SBM; so that SBM would become an international standard of value together with gold, into which SBM could be ultimately converted.

(*f*) SBM would rank equally with gold for the purposes of the legal reserves of the central banks in the scheme.

(*g*) The central banks would be expected to open accounts with the supranational bank by depositing a substantial sum of gold; thereafter their holdings of SBM would be replenished by further deposits of gold, by transfer of SBM from other central banks, and borrowing from the supranational bank.

(*h*) The supranational bank would decide on a bank rate at which the central banks could borrow from it for periods not exceeding three months at a time. The extent to which any central bank would be allowed to avail itself of these facilities would be determined by reference to the amount of that bank's average deposit with the supranational bank over (say) the previous three years, and initially by the amount of gold which it had deposited. For example, banks might be entitled to borrow initially up to an amount equal to that of their initial gold deposit, and after three years up to the amount of their average deposits over the previous three years. But the maximum permissible should, just like the bank rate, be subject to revision from time to time, according to the need to increase or to diminish the total quantity of SBM in the interests of its own

stability. Thus the supranational bank would control
the terms of credit to central banks in two ways —
through the bank rate and through the borrowing
limits. It would be desirable that the central banks
should make a practice of borrowing normally from
the supranational bank and not only in times of emergency.

(*i*) The supranational bank should also have the discretionary power to conduct open-market operations,
by the purchase or sale on its own initiative either of
long-term or short-term securities, with the consent, in
the case of a purchase, though not necessarily in the
case of a sale, of the central bank in whose national
money the securities in question are payable. There
would, however, be nothing to prevent the issue of
international loans in terms of SBM, and this might
tend in due course to become the usual practice. Thus
the supranational bank would eventually be free to
buy or sell entirely at its own discretion.

(*j*) The constitution of the bank is a matter of detail which
need not be discussed here. But presumably the
management would be independent, and have a high
degree of authority and discretion in daily management,
subject to the ultimate control of the Board of Super-
vision consisting of representatives of the central banks.

(*k*) Any profit the bank might make could be divided into
two parts, one of which would be placed to reserve,
and the other distributed to the central banks in
proportion to their average deposits.

(*l*) The principal objectives of the bank's management
would be two in number. It would be the first duty of
the management of the supranational bank to maintain,
so far as possible, the stability of the value of gold (or
SBM) in terms of a Tabular Standard based on the
principal articles of international commerce, as proposed above. Its second duty should be the avoidance,
so far as possible, of inflation and deflation of a general
international character. The methods by which these
ends would be attained would be partly through its
bank rate, its lending quotas and its open-market policy,

but also by consultation and joint action with and
between the central banks, who would be expected to
discuss their own credit policies at monthly meetings of
the Board of the supranational bank and to act, so far
as possible, on the lines jointly agreed upon.[1]

The supranational bank aimed at conducting international
control of credit through a centre, stabilizing the value of
international currency, as also the currencies of those countries
which are linked with it, and this without obstructing the
development of the world economy.

Keynes had also proposed,[2] as the second best measure,
the mutual granting of overdrafts between the central banks,
but he nevertheless thought that the establishment of the
supranational central bank was a better measure.

A Bank for International Settlements (BIS) for the handling
of German reparations had been set up about that time. This
bank, though it did not create an international currency,
received deposits from and made loans to the participating
central banks and bought and sold gold, foreign exchange and
negotiable securities. Keynes seems to have hoped that the
BIS would develop into such a supranational bank as he had
in mind, but his hopes were to be disappointed for the following reasons:

First, the Bank for International Settlements was set up for
the purpose of facilitating the transfer of gold in connection
with reparations and so, as this function by the passage of time
became non-existent, the bank lost its *raison d'être*.

Second, the bank's financial operations were not independent, being subject to the veto of the participating central
banks.

Third, the bank did not in fact, engage in current settlements.

Keynes approved the development of the BIS as a centre
in which the heads of the central banks could meet, and that
the smooth operation of the bank was shown to depend largely
upon the co-operation of the United States of America [3] may
be worthy of special notice in relation to subsequent events.

[1] J. M. Keynes, *A Treatise on Money*, pp. 395-402.
[2] *Ibid.* p. 311.   [3] *Ibid.* p. 405.

Furthermore, in March 1933 Keynes published an essay entitled 'The Means to Prosperity' in the London *Times*, in which he propounded the idea of an international organization issuing gold notes. It was designed to increase the supply of international currency and thereby increase international liquidity. As this plan has some connection with subsequent proposals, its main points are given below:

1. The participating countries would have their quotas fixed and, within their capacity, deliver gold bonds to an international organization.
2. The international organization would issue gold notes against the gold bonds, the face value of which would be expressed in that amount of gold being the equivalent to the U.S. dollar. The issue would be limited to a total of $5,000 million with a maximum limit for each quota of $450 million.
3. The participating countries would treat those notes as if they were gold and could hold them in their reserves.
4. The gold bond would be interest-bearing and redeemable at call. The notes would be used mainly for adjusting the level of prices of primary products and, therefore, the total issue and the level of interest rates would be fixed on the basis of the price level.
5. The limits of the official buying and selling prices for gold in the participating countries would be widened to 5 per cent subject to alteration in case of necessity. The currencies of all countries in the scheme could be exchanged for gold but not the gold notes.

In these proposals there are some points that deserve our attention. First, though the system is based on the gold standard, yet it is intended that these gold notes, which are for the time being divorced from gold, should be used as an international currency to increase liquidity. However, the backing for these gold notes is a corresponding issue of gold bonds. These gold notes, in that they cannot be converted into gold, are in sharp contrast to SBM, which are capable of being so converted, and it can be seen from this that as international currency, they are not in the same category as gold. What may be considered questionable, however, is that the limit for the fluctuation of exchange rates has been widened so much. Moreover, this limit itself is subject to change, should occasion arise, just as is the case with official rates. If a fixed rate be regarded as one of the indispensable features or advantages of the gold standard, then it is very doubtful whether the above system should be considered as a gold standard. Not only that, but the issue of gold bonds has the effect of creating credit facilities rather than that of providing an international currency, and, therefore, cannot be considered as a fundamental reform of the international currency system.

Next, the operation of the system is based upon the price level of primary products. Keynes on another occasion put forward a similar plan. In 1938, in his paper presented to the British Association for the Advancement of Science at its Cambridge meeting, he proposed the creation of buffer stocks of commodities. He proposed to accumulate stocks at a time of depression and, by releasing them in a boom, level out the extremes of the general business cycle.[1]

This is a parallel to White's proposal in his initial draft that a 'bank' should establish an 'International Commodity Stabilization Corporation' and provide its capital, so that the price of staple commodities could be stabilized.

It was against such a social and ideological background that Keynes published his *Proposals for an International Clearing Union* in April 1943.

Section 4.—The Keynes Plan

The Keynes Plan, like the White Plan, was only a draft and therefore had no definite form.

The Keynes Plan is, however, remarkably explanatory, so that the principles and recommendations of its author are quite clear.

We now propose to give below the main principles of the plan.

1. In its introduction, the Keynes Plan suggests that from the experience gained between the two wars, there are four ways of dealing with post-war economic problems.

---

[1] R. F. Harrod, *The Life of John Maynard Keynes*, pp. 532-3.

(*a*) The mechanism of currency and exchange.

(*b*) The framework of a commercial policy.

(*c*) Orderly organization of production, distribution and prices of primary products so as to protect both producers and consumers from the loss and risk brought about by the fluctuations of market conditions in recent times.

(*d*) Investment aid, both medium and long term, for countries whose economic development requires outside assistance.

It will be necessary to discuss all these matters in due course, but the plan itself only deals with (*a*).

2. For the creation of such a post-war international economic system, the plan suggests the following basic conditions:

(*a*) There should be the least possible interference with the internal policies of nations.

(*b*) The above principle should be applied to all countries whatever their political constitutions or regimes may be.

3. The management of the proposed system should be purely international and be of such a nature as to be able to protect the rights of small, and stand up to the pressure of great, nations.

4. Some qualification of the right to contract out of the plan would be required.

5. The plan should operate not only to the general advantage but also to the individual advantage of each of the participants, and therefore must not demand too great an economic or financial sacrifice from some of the countries in the plan.

In chapter i, detailed explanation is given of the objectives of the Clearing Union and main points are given in the following 1-4:

1. Nations should be given a guarantee that they would not be placed in such a position as to be driven to resort to bilateralism and direct control measures.

For this purpose it is necessary that the system should be in a position

(*a*) to offset inflationary and deflationary influences;

(*b*) to compel those countries, creditor or debtor, to adjust an imbalance of payments;

(c) to stabilize the value of all currencies;

(d) to constitute reserve funds for the purpose of increasing the degree of international liquidity (chapter i (b)-(e)).

2. Thus the plan proposes the creation of an international bank currency having a fixed (but not unalterable) value in terms of gold, to be called, say, Bancor, which should be accepted as the equivalent of gold by all member countries. The currencies of all the members should be linked with it at a certain fixed parity, but Bancor is a currency unit to be used solely by the central banks, and all transactions between private individuals, business firms, banks, other than the central banks, should use their own national currency as heretofore (chapter i, 1 (a) and 4).

3. The central banks of all member states (and also of non-members) would keep accounts with the International Clearing Union through which they would be entitled to settle their exchange balances with one another. Countries having a favourable balance of payments with the rest of the world as a whole would find themselves in possession of a credit account with the Clearing Union, and those having an unfavourable balance would have a debit account (chapter i, 4).

4. The idea is simple, namely, to generalize the essential principle of banking as it is practised within any closed system. This principle is the necessary equation of credits and debits. If credits cannot be transferred outside the clearing system, but only within it, the Union can never be in any difficulty in honouring cheques drawn upon it (chapter i, 5).

5. As, however, there is a danger of too great an accumulation of credit and debit accounts within the Union, chapter ii proposes the following regulations for the adjustment of any disequilibrium which may arise:

(a) Each member state shall be granted a quota, which shall determine the measure of its responsibility in the management of the Union and of its right to enjoy the credit facilities provided by the Union. The initial quotas might be calculated with reference to the total of each country's exports and imports averaged over the three pre-war years, and fixed at, say, 75 per cent of this amount. Subsequently, the quotas could be re-vised annually in accordance with the running average of each country's actual volume of trade in the three preceding years, rising to a five-year average when figures for five post-war years are available.

(*b*) A member shall pay to the Reserve Fund of the Clearing Union a charge of 1 per cent per annum on the amount of its average balance in Bancor, whether it is a credit or debit balance, in excess of a quarter of its quota; and a further charge of 1 per cent on its average balance, whether credit or debit, in excess of half of its quota.

(*c*) A member may not increase its debit balance by more than a quarter of its quota within a year without the permission of the Governing Board. If its debit balance has exceeded a quarter of its quota on the average of at least two years, it shall be entitled to reduce the value of its currency in terms of Bancor without the consent of the Governing Board, provided that the reduction does not exceed 5 per cent, but is not entitled to repeat this reduction unless the Board is satisfied that this procedure is appropriate.

(*d*) The Governing Board may require from a member the deposit of suitable collateral against its debit balance, should this reach half of its available quota. Such collateral shall, at the discretion of the Governing Board, take the form of gold, foreign or domestic currency or Government bonds.

(*e*) As a condition of allowing a member to increase its debit balance to a figure in excess of half its quota, the Governing Board may require the application of all or any of the following measures:

    (i) a reduction in the value of the member's currency, should it deem this to be suitable;

    (ii) the control of external capital transactions if not already in force;

    (iii) the outright surrender of a suitable proportion of any gold or other liquid reserves in reduction of its debit balance.

Furthermore, the Governing Board may recommend to the government of the member state any internal

The International Monetary Fund

measures affecting its domestic economy which may appear to be appropriate to the restoration of the equilibrium of its international balance.

(*f*) If a member's debit balance exceeds three-quarters of its quota on an average over at least a year, it may be asked by the Governing Board to take measures to improve its position, and, in the event of its failing to reduce its debit balance accordingly within two years, the Governing Board may declare that the member is in default and no longer entitled to draw against its account except with the permission of the Governing Board.

Each member state, on joining the system, shall agree to pay to the Clearing Union any payments due from it to a member in default towards the discharge of the latter's debit balance.

(*g*) A member whose credit balance has exceeded half of its quota on the average over at least a year shall discuss with the Governing Board (though any ultimate decision will be at its own discretion) what measures would be appropriate to restore the equilibrium of its international balance, including

   (i) Measures for the expansion of domestic credit and demand.
   (ii) The revaluation of its local currency in terms of Bancor, or, alternatively, the encouragement of an increase in earnings.
   (iii) The reduction of tariffs and other barriers to imports.
   (iv) International development loans.

(*h*) The Governing Board shall be entitled to reduce the quotas of members, all in the same specified proportion, if it should seem necessary to correct in this manner an excess of world purchasing power. If the Governing Board subsequently desires to correct a potential deficiency of world purchasing power, it shall be entitled to restore the general level of quotas to the original limits (chapter ii, 1-14).

As can be seen, the central principle of the Clearing Union is very simple. Keynes, however, wishing to lessen the apprehension of one of the creditor members to be (*i.e.* the United States of America), goes on to explain in detail the regulations for the adjustment of the above-mentioned disequilibrium, while enumerating minutely the advantages of the Union in chapters iii and iv. The outline of these chapters is given below :

6. While the growth of a debit balance is restricted in various ways, and the corrective measures are to be taken long before the maximum is reached, the accumulation of the credit balance is not subjected to such rigid requirements. Why?

   The first reason is that if strong rectifying measures are taken against credit balances accumulating in excess of a member's quota, it would result in too heavy a burden being placed upon the member, as such a surplus could only be rectified either by writing off the excess or requesting that it be compulsorily invested. (As stated later, in principle, it is impossible to convert a Bancor credit balance into gold.)

   If, on the other hand, the creditor member were to be precluded from accepting Bancor in excess of a prescribed figure, this might impair the general acceptability of Bancor, whilst at the same time conferring no real benefit on the creditor country itself. For, if it availed itself of this solution, the member must either restrict its exports or be driven back on to some form of bilateral payments agreement outside the Clearing Union (chapter vii).

7. It might therefore be feared that there would be the danger of a credit balance being accumulated endlessly, but this is not so, because a member country is entirely free to keep whatever balances it wishes in the Union. That is, a Bancor balance means nothing more than that the member country concerned holds within the Union, as long as it pleases, that external credit which it does not wish to hold elsewhere. Creditor members are under no restraint whatever as to how they employ their surplus receipts such as, for example, in making temporary external loans, or in the purchase of gold, etc.

   Thus, the effect of the Clearing Union is to give the creditor country a choice between voluntarily curtailing its

exports to the same extent that it would have been forced
to do in the absence of the Clearing Union, and, alternatively, allowing the flow of exports to continue unchecked
and accumulating the excess receipts in the form of Bancor
balances for the time being (chapter iii, 8, 9).

8. The advantage of the plan lies in that in world trade it
replaces the pressure for contraction by one of expansion.
This the plan intends to achieve by overdraft facilities
among its members, which, moreover, are automatically
made possible by the constitution of the system itself, and
do not give rise to any individual relationship between two
given countries.

For the accumulation of a credit balance with the Clearing
Union would resemble the importation of gold in that the
country concerned could be said to be voluntarily abstaining
from the immediate use of this purchasing power. The
importation of gold, however, would involve the withdrawal of this purchasing power from circulation, thus
exercising a deflationary pressure throughout the world.

The suggested provisions differ in one important respect
from the pre-war system, in that part of the responsibility
for adjustment is placed on the creditor country as well as
on the debtor. This is an attempt to recover one of the
advantages enjoyed in the nineteenth century, when a flow
of gold to London or Paris, the main creditor centres,
immediately produced an expansionist trend and increased
foreign lending in those markets (chapter iv, 10, 11, 17).

Keynes further emphasized in chapter v that his plan does not
obstruct either the freedom or the customary practice of international exchange transactions. His views are set out below:

9. The plan is a general payments agreement to restore un-
fettered multilateral clearing under which exchange dealings
would be carried on as freely as in the best days of the gold
standard, without the acceptance by anyone of any special
or onerous conditions (chapter v, 19, 20).

10. This means that the same procedure exerted under the
gold standard system, namely, the making of international
settlements through the shipment or the ear-marking of
gold between the central banks, is replaced by settlements

being made through the giving and taking of a Bancor balance as between the central banks (chapter v, 21).

11. The concentration or control of exchange exerted in all nations is in accord with the general purposes of the Union in that it would promote order and discipline in international exchange transactions, but this is not an indispensable condition. The Union does not seek to prevent private holdings of foreign currency or private dealings in exchange or in international capital movements, if these have been approved by the member States concerned. Central banks may deal direct with one another as heretofore (chapter v, 22).

12. The existence of the Union is not in contradiction to the continuation of such existing currency groups as, for example, the sterling area. It does not prevent the London or New York markets from functioning as the financial centre of such groups. Independent countries that are members of the groups are qualified for individual membership of the Union, but

   (*a*) there might be cases in which a dependency or a member of a group would not have a currency separate from that of the mother country, and would be included in the currency area as a whole. Such would not become separate individual members of the Clearing Union. And,

   (*b*) in order that sterling and dollars might not appear to compete with Bancor for the purpose of reserve balances, the United Kingdom and the United States should agree together that they would not accept the reserve balances of other countries in excess of normal working balances except in the case of banks belonging to a sterling area or dollar area group (chapter v, 23-25).

Furthermore, Keynes referred in chapter vi and in other places to the important position gold is given in the Union.

13. Gold still possesses great psychological value which is not diminished by current events; and the desire to possess a gold reserve against unforeseen contingencies is likely to continue. Gold also has the merit (whatever the underlying realities may be) of providing an uncontroversial

standard of value for international purposes, for which no serviceable substitute has yet been found. Moreover, the current gold production of the world and the gold reserves held outside the United States may still have a useful part to play. What, in the long run, the world may decide to do about gold is another matter. The purpose of the Clearing Union is to supplant gold as a governing factor, but not to dispense with it altogether (chapter vi, 26).

14. The central banks should not deal in gold at a price exceeding their parity (chapter vi, 28).

15. A member state shall be entitled to obtain a credit in terms of Bancor by paying in gold to the credit of its clearing account with the Clearing Union; no member is, however, entitled to demand from the Union gold against a balance of Bancor, since this balance is available only for transfer to another clearing account. The Governing Board may, however, at their discretion, distribute proportionately any gold in the possession of the Union amongst the members possessing credit balances in excess of a specified proportion of their quotas, in reduction of that excess (chapter ii, 10).

Thus, there would be a one-way convertibility between gold and Bancor as happened frequently before the war with national currencies which were on the so-called 'gold exchange standard'. This need not mean that the Clearing Union would never pay out but only receive gold (chapter vi, 29).

In chapter vii Keynes touches upon the control of the movement of capital, including the treatment of blocked balances. His main provisions are as follows:

16. The active movement of capital based upon speculation, or seeking a haven of safety, is expected to continue and it therefore becomes necessary to control it. This, however, is not indispensable. Further advocacy of the control of capital movements must not be taken to mean that international investment should cease (chapter vii, 32, 33, 35).

17. The abnormal balances in overseas ownership held in various countries at the end of the war present an im-

portant and specially difficult problem. A country holding a large balance of this nature could not, unless it were in a creditor position, afford the risk of having to redeem them in Bancor on a substantial scale, if this would have the effect of depleting its Bancor resources (chapter vii, 34).

18. The machinery and organization of international medium-term and long-term lending is another aspect of post-war economic policy, no less important than that of the Clearing Union, but requiring the establishment of another and complementary institution.

In chapters viii and ix, it is emphasized that the Union should be capable of acting in support of commercial and other policies. For example, the Union, by co-operating with the Board for International Investment and operating the Bancor accounts of the countries concerned, could act as its agent.

The Union would also advance funds to create buffer stocks in connection with commodities subject to control.

It is because of its 'anonymous' or 'impersonal' character that the Union is so suited for such international activities (chapter ix, 40).

Lastly, in chapter x and the conclusion, Keynes points out that though the expanding character of the Union is likely to be inflationary in the post-war transitional period, yet, when that period is over, such a character will be of advantage to the Union, and he insists that 'We must not be over-cautious'. He also insists that the post-war world will need to engage in a so-called financial disarmament, by which is meant the relinquishment by all members of such of their freedom as is required to prevent lack of control, disorder and unneighbourly action. He concludes that the plan constitutes the first step toward economic order and 'the winning of the peace'.

It will be seen, therefore, that the most important feature of the Keynes Plan is the creation of an international banking currency named Bancor, which is automatically brought into existence through the operations and functions of the Union.

Thus, should a member country find itself with an excess

of imports over exports, which excess it cannot cover from other resources, it can automatically obtain an overdraft from the Union, the amount of which is transferred to the account of one or more other countries.

Let us take the case of three member countries, A, B and C. A and B have a credit balance of 5 each while country C has a debit balance of 10. A change in the payments position between countries A and B leads to the disappearance of the credit balance of country B and an increase to 10 of that of country A. The current situation is that now only country A has given credit to country C, not A and B as previously was the case. The debit position of country C, however, is entirely unrelated to this change, which is, indeed, the reason why the Union is called 'anonymous' or 'impersonal'. Moreover, in this case, the responsibility of country A is limited to the amount of Bancor it has not used. Thus no creditor country can insist upon any special advantages, all countries enjoying an equal status.

Let us now explain the relation between such settlements between central banks and exchange settlements between commercial banks.

If, for example, a given country's exports exceed its imports, a *surplus* of foreign exchange on its exchange markets will result. This surplus is sold by an exchange bank to the monetary authorities and thus forms part of that country's official foreign exchange reserves. The foreign currency thus accumulated by the authorities is sold to the Union for Bancor at a previously fixed parity, instead of being exchanged for gold to be paid by the debtor country (in the case of U.S. dollars, the United States of America). The Bancor thus acquired is credited to that country's account with the Union. The foreign currency obtained in this way by the Union is debited in Bancor (if there is no balance, as an overdraft) to the account of the debtor country with the Union and automatically cleared, thus avoiding a settlement in gold by the debtor country, that is, the country that has issued that currency (in the case of U.S. dollars, the United States of America). If, on the other hand, a given country's imports exceed its exports, a *shortage* of foreign currency will arise on its exchange market.

Such a shortage is eventually made good from the official

foreign currency reserves of the authorities concerned. The foreign currency thus required is bought from the Union for Bancor (that is, the Bancor account of the country concerned is debited, and, should there be no balance, an overdraft is created) while the Union for its part buys the foreign currency required from the country which issued that currency (the United States of America in the case of U.S. dollars), not by a settlement in gold but, through automatic clearing, by crediting the Bancor account of the issuing country.

For this system to work, the creditor country must agree to receive a Bancor deposit instead of gold in settlement of its foreign currency credit, and this Bancor deposit, though it cannot be exchanged for gold, may be exchanged for any of the required currencies under the above-mentioned system. Therefore, the accumulation of Bancor deposits is just as effective as gold as a reserve for international settlements. The compulsion to accept such deposits, Keynes thinks, does not inflict any special burden on the receiving country. As a Bancor deposit may be freely exchanged for any other currency, it is unnecessary for the national authorities concerned to hold reserves in those foreign currencies whose rates fluctuate frequently, and thus the greater part of foreign currency holdings would be converted into Bancor deposits, whose value is stable (at least, for a certain period of time). In this way, the international currency system, which has hitherto included the domestic currency of other countries as well as gold in its reserves, can now be converted into a system that has Bancor deposits as reserves, which are in effect international currency. At the same time, through the creation of Bancor, the way is clear for a surprisingly large increase in world reserves.

The plan for the creation of Bancor, however, has one great drawback in spite of the advocacy of Keynes. It is the size of the creative power of Bancor. According to Keynes, international settlements are carried out through the lending, borrowing or transfer of Bancor deposits, and, as already mentioned, Bancor received in settlement cannot be exchanged for gold.

In consequence, theoretically speaking, the granting by the Union of Bancor loans may be compared to a country issuing inconvertible notes thereby creating limitless domestic credit, and without any gold reserves. According to the Keynes Plan, it is true, fixed quotas are established and a debtor country may obtain a Bancor loan only within the scope of its own fixed quota, but there are no measures to control credit balances, though there are some regarding debit balances. While the responsibility of a creditor country under the White Plan is limited to the amount of its subscription quota, the position of a creditor country under the Keynes Plan depends wholly upon the situation and attitude of debtor countries.

To take an extreme case, there is the possibility of the accumulation of credit balances of one creditor country being equal to the total of the quotas of all debtor countries. Further, as these quotas are to be periodically revised (see 5), it may be said that there is no limit at all. This, however, is one of the advantages of the Keynes Plan. Under the White Plan, which is an open system, there is the danger that the currencies of creditor countries may be exhausted long before all the demands of debtor countries are satisfied. Under the Union Plan, however, Bancor is not used for any purpose other than Union settlement, and, as it is a closed system, such a situation as mentioned above could not happen until the amount reaches the total of the quotas of all debtor members, and this is one of the distinct advantages of the plan.

During the anticipated post-war dollar shortage, however, such an extreme case as the one cited above could not be dismissed off-hand as fantasy. To put it more positively, the amount of the resources of the Union was estimated from the value of world trade at that time to be about $26 billion, of which $23 billion, the balance remaining after deduction of the American quota, were to be equal to the total drawing rights of the other participating countries.

In an extreme case, therefore, there was a possible danger of the United States of America being required to make un-requited exports to that amount.

At any rate, one characteristic feature of the plan lies in its self-balancing gold-standard-like capacity of preventing the tendency of creditor countries to hoard their surplus from international settlements in gold and thus reducing to that extent international liquidity, and of imposing an adjustment of their structural imbalance even upon creditor countries which keep their credit in Bancor balances for the purpose of international settlements.

In some cases, however, there is a danger of creating an infinite excess of expansion.

A second feature, bearing upon the above, concerns the question of exchange rates under the plan. The plan recognizes as valid a change of parity as a measure for rectifying an unbalanced position, as also a change in the gold value of Bancor, should the occasion arise.

Keynes even goes further, saying in effect: Should the levels of wages and commodity prices of a given country expressed in currency become unbalanced when compared with those of other countries, then a change in its exchange rate becomes unavoidable (chapter vi, 18).

In effect, under the Keynes Plan, exchange rates should be varied when control is necessary and not be fixed; in this respect the White Plan is more rigid. Keynes does not regard the stabilization of rates of exchange as such an important factor, in that when a certain degree of domestic stabilization has been secured, a change of parity may be considered as a means of adjusting the external situation to agree with it. This may be the natural reaction due to a view that places more emphasis upon growth than upon stabilization, and more stress upon domestic than upon external equilibrium. (Nothing is said of the limits of the change of exchange rates, but we shall touch upon this later.)

The third question is gold. The gold value of Bancor is controlled by the Union and, in consequence, gold is controlled by Bancor. Between gold and Bancor there is only a one-way traffic, which means the encouragement of the expanding character of gold and the suppression of its deflationary aspects; this is in keeping with the views of Keynes for expansionism as expressed in other parts of the plan. Keynes asserts that the necessity for a one-way traffic is based upon the fear that if free exchange be permitted, it would be necessary to hold gold reserves against Bancor and thus lead back to the situation previously existing.[1]

Generally, there is no doubt that Keynes predicated the

[1] J. M. Keynes, 'The International Clearing Union' (S. E. Harris, *The New Economics*).

dethronement of gold from its pinnacle, but even he could not ignore the hard fact that, in the present situation, gold is, fundamentally, an international currency, and he had therefore to compromise where gold was concerned wherever he met it. This is the reason why the basis of the value of Bancor was sought in gold, and why an attempt was made to apportion gold among debtor countries, thus violating the principle of one-way traffic. Besides, the Union, being a steady and reliable buyer, was obliged to protect the position of gold-producing countries.

Because of its inconclusive character, the Keynes Plan, as pointed out by Lutz, could make possible the following curious situation. Suppose that the United States of America, by mobilizing its gold holdings, had put into practice inflationary policies. As its balance of payments deteriorated, it would become a debtor country within the Union. It would then have to sell gold to the Union and thereby replenish its Bancor. Thus the Union, as a whole, might be placed in the position that it held an enormous amount of Bancor backed by gold in addition to the Bancor resulting from the quotas and the superfluity of liquidity. Thereupon, the Union would have to resort to a wholesale reduction of quotas for the purpose of maintaining confidence in Bancor (see 5 (*h*)), and this in an extreme case might lead to the position in which only Bancor backed by gold remained, the Bancor resulting from the quotas having been eliminated. In other words, the function of creating currency through the Union will have been lost, resulting in the revival of the gold standard.[1] Thus, in spite of the one-way convertibility of Bancor, there would be a return to the past state of affairs.

The fourth question concerns relations with the existing exchange controls and currency blocs. Keynes says that his plan is designed to promote free exchange transactions and not to obstruct them ; but there is no doubt that the concentration of exchange in the central banks would be more likely to increase the volume passing through the Union than otherwise, as is explained in the latter half of chapter xxii (see 11 above). Unless exchange is concentrated in the accounts of the central banks, it cannot be brought into Bancor settlements.

[1] G. N. Halm, *International Monetary Co-operation*, pp. 148-9.

Though the plan does not touch upon the limits of changes in exchange rates, it is clear that, the greater the limits, the wider would be the scope for settlements between commercial banks. The imbalance of international payments would be absorbed by the market and the necessity therefore for Bancor settlements would decrease. Though it is natural that a floating rate should lessen the necessity of a gold settlement (corresponding to a Bancor settlement), on this matter something can be learned from the experience of the European Payments Union (EPU), which was, as it were, a continental version of the plan. The EPU adopted the principle of parity for its settlements, and this was possible because at first there was no exchange market; even after one existed, the limit of change in the rates was limited to as narrow a margin as 0·75 per cent on each side of parity. Even then, it was impossible to prevent the central bank of a member country from buying from commercial banks the currencies of other countries which were weak and bringing them in for EPU settlement at parity. With the winding up of the EPU and the institution of the European Monetary Agreement (EMA), the range of exchange rates was broadened and the principle of parity abandoned, the aim being to cultivate and reinforce the exchange market together with the restoration of the convertibility of currencies. It was therefore difficult to maintain the principle of parity. As a result, the multilateral settlement organization of EMA seems to have become nominal. Under the Keynes Plan, settlements within the Union are based upon the principle of parity, but there is no clear explanation of the relationship between these settlements and market rates and between exchange markets and the functions of the Union in that field. If multilateral settlement worked efficiently, there would be no need of flexible rates, but if flexible rates are adopted, the necessity for multilateral settlements will diminish.

In this connection, the coexistence of a currency bloc, such as the sterling area, with the organization of the plan would be quite natural as far as Britain is concerned, but it is doubtful whether such coexistence is possible, for the stronger the desire for the maintenance of such international financial centres as London or New York, the less would the function of the Union be. Moreover, it is questionable whether the advantages

77

resulting from participation in the Union would alone be a
sufficient incentive for countries to cease the accumulation of
dollar or sterling balances outside the Union. This question is
justified because chapter v of the plan advocates that international centres should abstain from taking deposits of international currencies as much as possible.

In short, the plan may be said to be contradictory in that,
if it insists upon active use being made of the organization of
the Union, it will have to play down the abolition of parity
and discourage the practice of exchange discrimination but,
if it advocates little use being made of the organization, it will
have to encourage the former and approve of discrimination.

Apart from this, it is quite clear that the plan intends the
Union to be an international financial centre and at the same
time act as an artificial exchange settlement centre, playing
the role of a world central bank both in name and in fact by
the creation of an international currency and the control of
gold and credit. And the controllers are, in fact, two, the
United States of America and Britain. Thus, in contrast to
the White Plan, which intended to establish a dollar standard
system with the United States as controller with Unitas as its
agent, this plan may be said to intend bringing about the
establishment of an international currency system influenced
by the pound standard. In this sense, Bancor is thus not a
new international currency, but the agent of the pound and
the dollar. This may be regarded as a further development
in another form of the idea Keynes entertained for so long,
namely that of the control of international finance through
collaboration between the United States and Britain.

Section 5.—Compromise between two Plans : Signing of the Bretton Woods Agreements

It was only to be expected that the foregoing plans evolved
by the United States and Britain should give rise to heated
discussions in government and other circles in these two
countries. To recall those discussions and to examine the way
in which the present IMF system was evolved as a result of
those discussions and of the compromise that was reached, is

indispensable in order to understand its character and the problems it had to solve.

In Britain, the gold-standard character of the White Plan evoked serious apprehension, for it was regarded as not in keeping with its expansionist policies, nor with its desire to establish a welfare state. Objections were chiefly raised to the fixed rates, shortage of funds and lack of full control over creditor countries which were inherent in the proposed stabilization fund.

In the United States, on the other hand, strong dissatisfaction was expressed, as was expected, at the expansionist character of the Keynes Plan. This dissatisfaction was directed against the principles of the Plan themselves. The *New York Times* looked upon Keynes as an antagonist of stable exchange rates and as a champion of devaluation and credit expansion. Picking on the planning aspect of his plan, it argued that the Clearing Union was a 'machine for the regimentation of the world'.

Furthermore, the isolationists, many of whom reside in the United States, refused to participate in any international organizations, including that envisaged by the White Plan. Opposition also came from those who feared foreign interference in the domestic economy. The conservatives considered the two plans 'dangerous', because both of them were designed to carry out an adjustment of the balance of payments and exchange rates, not by means of impersonal market forces, but on the basis of an 'often-erroneous and artificial judgment'.

In September 1943, a British delegation consisting of financial experts including Keynes, visited the United States, and after discussions over several months, a 'Joint Statement by Experts on the Establishment of an International Monetary Fund' was issued.

This statement contained almost all the main clauses that were later adopted in the International Monetary Fund Agreement, and, despite the opposition of Keynes, was fundamentally based upon the White Plan, with only some of the features of the Keynes Plan. It was a compromise between the two plans, the Keynes Plan itself having been dropped in the initial stages of the negotiations.

Prior to this, in November 1943, the United States proposed the establishment of a world bank, but it is said that this proposal did not receive much attention from the British until two or three weeks before the Bretton Woods Conference.

It is interesting to note how Britain, which had been compelled to make great concessions in favour of the White Plan, attempted to recover lost ground, because this has some connection with later developments.

First, there was the question of liquidity. As stated earlier, the Keynes Plan permits overdraft facilities amounting to at least $26 billion. As a result, the potential burden of the United States could conceivably amount to as much as $23 billion. The Americans, therefore, insisted that this should not be allowed, saying that it would 'change the United States into a milch cow'. This insistence was based upon the argument that $2-3 billion at most should be the limit of its subscription, and that the payment of a subscription which exceeded that sum and whose limit was unknown but was fixed automatically through the mechanism of a Clearing Union, was tantamount to a violation of the legislative power of Congress, and therefore, such a subscription would never be approved by Congress. Thus (in the final agreement of the Bretton Woods Conference) the subscription of the United States was fixed at $2,750 million.

Keynes now endeavoured to obtain an agreement that would enable member countries to draw on IMF funds unconditionally. The White Plan, however, has no provision for unconditional drawing. Further, many people in the United States were of the opinion that the control even under the White Plan was not sufficient.

The compromise on this point finally took the form of a general conditional clause in the Joint Statement, chapter iii, 2 (*a*) to the effect that the member concerned should affirm that the currency it desires to purchase is required for making payments in that currency which are consistent with the purposes of the Fund. This clause was also incorporated in the IMF Agreement.

It was further provided, however, that, should a member country make use of funds from the Fund contrary to its purposes, it would be possible to limit the member's drawing on the Fund (chapter v, 5). Regarding drawings on the Fund, whether limited or not, the regulations are not as clear as might be desirable.

The second point is the adjustment of an imbalance. As regards the alteration of an exchange parity, it has already been stated that, in the White Plan, there is a very strict regulation to the effect that it should only be considered if it be necessary to correct a fundamental disequilibrium. The British, however, demanded greater freedom for a change of par value. In consequence, the Joint Statement contains a negative regulation to the effect that it is not for the Fund to judge the question of a change, but that the member country concerned should not propose a change if there is no fundamental disequilibrium. This clause has become part of the IMF Agreement. What is more important is that the IMF Agreement provides that 'the Fund shall concur in a proposed change if it is satisfied that the change is necessary to correct a fundamental disequilibrium', and, provided it is so satisfied, 'it shall not object to the proposed change because of the domestic, social, or political policies of the member proposing the change'.

The principle of non-interference in domestic affairs, as already stated, has been consistently insisted upon by the British since the Keynes Plan.

Under the original White Plan, the stabilization fund could request a debtor country to rectify its imbalance, but in the published plan this request was worded in a far more roundabout way. Even that has now gone, and, as a result, it is no longer possible for the IMF to formulate any conditions for a change in par value. The authority of the Fund therefore has been to that extent diminished.

Then, at the Bretton Woods Conference, the American side returned to their previous contention, as a result of which they succeeded in having Article VII, Section 8, inserted into the IMF Agreement reading as follows: 'The Fund shall at all times have the right to communicate its views informally to any member on any matter arising under this Agreement'.

The second point regarding the rectification of external disequilibrium is the so-called scarce currency clause. Though there is no doubt that this clause is a measure for the control of a creditor country to take the place of automatic overdraft facilities, Keynes is said to have at first been rather sceptical. Later he tried to expand the clause. In the Joint Statement, however, the right of the stabilization fund to make a recommendation to a creditor country, and the obligation of member countries of paying speedy and careful attention to the recommendation, both provided for in the White Plan, have been dropped, and the participating countries have been given complete freedom to determine the nature of their limitations on foreign exchange operations. That is another way of saying that the independent character of the Fund has been much reduced. In the IMF Agreement, however, it is specifically stated that scarcity can only be an established fact when the Fund has made an official declaration to that effect and, as a result, member countries may temporarily apply exchange restrictions to scarce currency countries. This provision may indeed have been the result of efforts on the part of the British delegation.

The practical effect of this provision, however, is limited to those cases 'when it becomes evident to the Fund that the demand for a member's currency seriously threatens the Fund's ability to supply that currency' (IMF Agreement, chapter vii, section 3 (*a*)), and, therefore, is of dubious value, since, even though the currency concerned has become scarce outside the fund, that fact alone will not lead to any action unless such a situation arises within the Fund. In such cases, of course, demands on the Fund for the currency concerned could be expected to be heavy, but the Fund will be able to counteract such pressure through its operational measures. Such a situation, as will be explained later, actually arose in the post-war period of dollar shortage. Moreover, with the possibility of pressure by the Fund upon creditor countries thus curtailed, the clause under review was in danger of being rendered inoperative.

The third point is the question of the post-war transitional period. It was quite natural that Britain, a country stricken by war, should have been greatly interested, but she could not easily agree to the abolition of exchange restrictions unless some support or assistance were provided. Though a proposal for a world bank was put forward with this situation in mind,

Britain could not help feeling that a subscription of an enormous amount to the 'bank' in addition to one to the Fund, was of little advantage, if any. Eventually, the initial payment to the bank was limited to 20 per cent of the total and to 2 per cent of the total for that part which was to be paid in gold or U.S. dollars.

On the other hand, Britain could not obtain from the Fund a guarantee of aid for the transitional period, and this was left to be dealt with later in a British-American financial agreement. Britain did succeed, however, in having a new clause inserted concerning a transitional matter, by which it was resolved that the agreement of a member country to those provisions regarding the restoration of currency convertibility, abolition of restrictions upon current international transactions, elimination of discriminative currency agreements and multiple currency measures, 'should not become operative until the Fund is satisfied as to the arrangements at that country's disposal to facilitating the settlement of balance of payments differences during the early post-war transitional period by means which will not unduly encumber its facilities with the Fund' (Joint Statement, chapter x, 1). Moreover, it was decided that member countries shall undertake to withdraw progressively any restrictions as soon as possible (chapter x, 2), and that 'any member still retaining any restrictions shall consult with the Fund as to their further retention not later than three years after the coming into force of the Fund' (chapter x, 3) and that 'the Fund shall recognize that the transition period is one of change and adjustment, and in deciding on its attitude to any proposal presented by members it shall give them the benefit of any reasonable doubt' (chapter x, 4). Further, all the clauses concerning the treatment of blocked balances provided for in the White Plan were dropped.

This Joint Statement gave rise to vigorous discussion, not only in Britain and the United States, but also in other countries. First of all, in order to judge of the reaction in Britain, we give hereunder the comparison made between the Joint Statement and the Keynes Plan in the White Paper published by the British Government:

1. While, in the Clearing Union, the Union becomes the bank of its member countries and they open accounts with it,

in the 'Fund', the member countries become the banks of the 'Fund', as a result of which a member's drawing upon the Union brings about a decrease in the fund account of the country concerned and an increase in its accounts in other countries, while in the 'Fund' it increases the account of that country in the 'Fund' and decreases its accounts in other countries. These two methods are of a similar function and so either of them may be resorted to.

2. In consequence, in the 'Fund' there is no need of any new international currency such as Bancor or Unitas, because an international currency unit is only required when members effect a banking transaction with the 'Fund'.

3. Only central banks of member countries can operate with the Union, while the treasury as well as the central banks may deal with the 'Fund'.

4. The total payment facilities given against the quota are smaller in the 'Fund' than in the Union, but are still considerable and, moreover, can be increased should necessity arise.

5. The Clearing Union plan is critized as lacking in proper control of the elasticity of exchange rates and of their fluctuations. In view of this criticism, the 'Fund' laid down clear regulations regarding a change in the par value. However, it adheres to the general principle that a change in a par value should be subject to international consultation. Any member country, unable to agree to any decision on the above made by the 'Fund', is free to withdraw from it.

6. Apart from temporary exceptions, the provisions designed to establish the convertibility of currencies, involve, after all, the same principle in the 'Fund' and in the Clearing Union.

7. The responsibility of maintaining the convertibility of currencies is limited to current transactions and is not applicable to capital transactions nor to the movement of funds accumulated prior to the acceptance of the responsibility of maintaining currency convertibility. It is also provided that member countries should not make use of the 'Fund' for an enormous or a continuous outflow of capital. The 'Fund' therefore recognizes exchange control within certain limits.

8. The proposal incorporated in the Clearing Union, for the purpose of preventing the speedy dissipation of their quotas by the member countries and their drawing on the Fund in spite of holding sufficient funds of their own, has been adopted for the 'Fund' in a more elaborated form. The regulations that member countries should pay part of their quotas in gold or gold exchange, and that which relates to the acquisition of gold by the 'Fund', are new. Under the latter the 'Fund' is prepared to hold some gold, increase its holding gradually, and use it freely to secure equilibrium in international finance.

9. That provision had been made for pressure to be exerted on both debtor and creditor countries, to force them to bear the responsibility of maintaining the stability of their balances of payments, is one of the characteristics of the Clearing Union, but the 'Fund' in this connection is more precise.

Thus, in the event of a particular currency becoming scarce, the 'Fund' must issue a report on the causes of the excess of receipts over payments of the country whose currency is scarce, as well as the measures to be taken for rectifying the position. At the same time, the 'Fund' should apportion the currency that is scarce, and the other members would recover their freedom of action for imposing restrictions upon imports, exchange and the like in regard to the scarce currency country.

10. The proposals governing the basic principles of the 'Fund' do not lay down detailed regulations for the management of its institutions.

11. The proposal for the Clearing Union was elaborated comparatively early and so did not deal fully with the measures required to be taken during the post-war transitionary period, but the 'Fund' proposals had made some progress in this direction, as the provisions of chapter x are with that intent. As a result, the experts of both the United States and Britain were agreed that the maintenance and amendment of those existing exchange arrangements between the sterling area countries meant for the transitional period were entirely justified. Further the 'Fund' system is not designed to interfere in the

traditional connections and arrangements between the sterling area countries and Britain.

12. On other matters, there is practically no difference between the plans for the Union and the 'Fund'.

A glance at the above shows that the White Paper has intentionally been ambiguous about the fundamental difference between the Union and the 'Fund'. Thus, in (1) it touches only upon the manner in which funds are provided, but states that the two methods are of a similar character and so can both be used, and in (4) deals only with the size of the credit facilities and avoids any reference to their difference. However, it is obvious that the fundamental difference between the two lies in whether the credit facilities are automatic or not. Moreover, the White Paper, in (5), casually says that if any member country is dissatisfied with the level of exchange rates insisted upon by the 'Fund', it can withdraw from it; but this assertion in the White Paper entirely ignores the position under post-war circumstances, which makes it practically impossible for any of the free countries participating in the system to leave it so easily.

To say that the clause concerning scarce currency in the 'Fund' is stronger as a measure for the control of creditor countries than the self balancing capacity of the Clearing Union, is theoretically right, as Mrs. Joan Robinson points out (see Chapter V, section 2 of this book), but, as has already been pointed out, its practical effects are dubious, depending on how it is carried out. It also is an exaggeration to say that the IMF is freely able to use the gold in its possession.

The reason why the White Paper was obliged to assume such a persuasive attitude was that, at the time, antipathy towards multilateralism was a growing force in Britain. Further, the fact that the new plan was a 'monetary fund proposal' revived the suspicion that it would mean a return to the gold standard, and stimulated the natural apprehension that such an international financial organization would constitute the recognition of dependence upon the economic fortunes of foreign countries, especially of the United States, and of priority being given to external equilibrium.

Moreover, the City was strongly of the opinion that participation in such an organization was against the interests of the London market, and the Bank of England feared that the leadership in international finance would pass from London and that sterling exchange would be replaced by the dollar. From the very beginning, the Bank of England on the whole also cold-shouldered the Keynes Plan, which, it is said, was one of the causes of its lack of success, and it did so presumably because it feared that the appearance of a supra-central bank such as the IMF would result in the decline of its powers of controlling credit on the London market.

Thereupon, Keynes, in the House of Lords on 23 May 1944, made a defence of its proposed principles with a view to clarifying the purpose of the 'Fund'. As, however, he himself was perhaps unwilling to recommend the 'Fund' proposal, his manner of delivery seemed rather hesitant and his reasoning somewhat far-fetched. His speech was, however, an important example of the way the British received the 'Fund' proposal; it may not be amiss therefore to examine it in some detail.[1]

First of all, Keynes honestly deplored the demise of the Clearing Union saying: 'There were, it is true, certain features of elegance, clarity, and logic in the Clearing Union plan which have disappeared. And this, to me at least, is to be much regretted,' but, continuing, he found there were some compensating factors: 'I still think that it was a more thorough-bred animal than what has now come out from a mixed marriage of ideas. Yet, perhaps, as sometimes occurs, this dog of mixed origin is a sturdier and more serviceable animal and will prove not less loyal and faithful to the purposes for which it has been bred.'

He then enumerated the following five advantages of the new plan:

First, it has given Britain the assurance that there is no objection to Britain continuing its various kinds of war-time controls and arrangements 'during the post-war transitional period of uncertain duration'.

Second, when this period is past, the new plan is not

[1] J. M. Keynes, 'The International Monetary Fund' (S. E. Harris, *The New Economics*, pp. 369-79.)

incompatible with the sterling system. We shall again soon attain convertibility and see London used by the Commonwealth and other countries as the traditional financial centre of the sterling system. The plan does not endanger this tradition. It may even be said to be indispensable for its maintenance.

Third, the plan increases by quota and distributes rationally such currency as is necessary for the smooth working of world trade. Though the quota is not as large in amount as in the Clearing Union, yet it is still considerable and, if necessary, is capable of being increased two or three fold. In these difficult times, is there anyone who can be so confident of the future as to refuse such favourable supplementary assistance?

Fourth, it should especially be noticed that under the plan creditor countries as well must bear, in fairness, part of the responsibility for maintaining international monetary equilibrium. This is one of the main improvements of the new plan. (Referring, no doubt, to the apportionment of scarce currency in the Joint Statement, chapter vi.)

Fifth, the plan establishes an international organization for making orderly agreements and offers a forum for regular discussions between the parties concerned.

Keynes, replying to the apprehension that the plan might mean a return to the gold standard, says: 'If I have any authority to pronounce on what is and what is not the essence and meaning of a gold standard, I should say that this plan is the exact opposite to it'. And he further says that, as for the plan making gold a basis of value of currency, it is 'using gold merely as a convenient common denominator by means of which the relative values of national currencies are expressed from time to time. And so long as gold is used as a monetary reserve, it is most advisable that the current rates of exchange and the relative values of gold in different currencies should correspond. The only alternative to this would be the complete demonetization of gold. I am not aware that anyone has proposed that. For it is only common sense as things are today to continue to make use of gold and its prestige as a means of settling international accounts.'

In reply to the important question as to who decides the value of gold Keynes explains : 'that if it means the sterling value of gold, it is ourselves who fix it in consultation with the Fund. It is always capable of being changed on our proposal.' On this point, he also says : 'instead of maintaining the principle that the internal value of a national currency should conform to a prescribed *de jure* external value, the plan provides that its external value should be altered if necessary so as to conform to whatever *de facto* internal value results from domestic policies'. 'Indeed, it is made the duty of the Fund to approve changes which will have this effect.' 'Yet a not less difficult task still remains — namely, to organize an international setting within which the new domestic policies can occupy a comfortable place. Therefore, it is above all as providing an international framework for the new ideas and the new techniques associated with the policy of full employment that those proposals are not least to be welcomed.'

It is clear that this statement of Keynes is of a very political nature. Intentionally or not, his explanation stressed the essential prerequisite of the freedom of changing exchange parities, the automatism of the use of funds and the effectiveness of the scarce currency clause. It is very doubtful whether the Americans were of the same opinion on these important points.

Be that as it may, despite his efforts, there were many who were not convinced that multilateralism and traditional regionalism could exist together, and dissension continued. Even after the middle of 1945, there was no definite British opinion. Finally, toward the end of that year, the British decided to approve the agreement on condition that a loan of $3,750 million were granted to Britain in accordance with the Anglo-American Financial Agreement.

Prior to this, on 1 July 1944 a United Nations Monetary and Financial Conference was held at Bretton Woods, New Hampshire, in the United States, in which the representatives of 44 Allied countries took part, the subjects for discussion being the main principles of the above-mentioned Joint Statement and World Bank plan. After about three weeks of close discussion, the proposals for the 'Fund' and the 'Bank' were adopted, and the conference came to an end on the 22nd of the same month. The result of the work of the conference was known as 'Final Act of the United Nations Monetary and Financial Conference' with two appendices 'Agreement of the International Monetary Fund' and 'Agreement of the International Bank for Reconstruction and Development'. These two agreements are generally known as the Bretton Woods Agreements, and the two organizations, the 'Fund' and the 'Bank' themselves, are generally called the Bretton Woods Organizations.

Meanwhile, in the United States, these agreements were the subject of intensive discussion. Though the American Administration presented the texts of the two agreements to Congress for approval in January 1945, this approval was not easy to obtain.

The chief objection raised in the United States was that for that country, a creditor nation, to grant loans to such an international organization, would be contrary to the healthy business principles of a capitalistic society. According to the usual principles of lending and borrowing, the borrower should be known, and the conditions for the loan should be fixed according to his credit standing.

But a loan to this international organization meant financing an indefinite number of other parties for an indefinite use. The right of deciding the conditions of the loan is entirely in the hands of the international organization. Not only that, but the United States has little power of control in the organization in spite of its very large subscription. It was just like 'pouring money down a rat hole' (as Senator Taft said). This was the gist of the arguments of the isolationists and financiers in the United States.[1] Thus did private conservatives and business leaders commence their counter-attack against the principle of international planning as proposed by the Administration (Chapter V, Section 1).

There was the further American argument that the provisions for the stabilization of exchange rates and the abolition of exchange restrictions were not sufficient.

Voices were also raised against the scarce currency clause, which it was asserted had the effect of putting the responsibility for adjustment entirely upon the creditor nations, and left the door open for the dangerous possibility of interference in internal affairs.

[1] Richard N. Gardner, *Sterling-Dollar Diplomacy*, 1956, p. 130.

The point which evoked the greatest number of objections was that these plans did not clearly show how they were going to cope with the situation during the post-war transitional period.

The objectors asserted that the Bretton Woods organization was a long-term formula of little use in the transitional period. Despite that, the view was prevalent that it would also be efficient for that purpose. Whatever form it might take, an international financial organization could not function unless it was based upon a certain degree of economic world equilibrium. In the field of currency, such an organization could not be expected to function smoothly in a situation where, on the one hand, there was an enormous demand from a number of countries for a specific international currency while, on the other, there was a limit to the supply of that specific currency. The question was, therefore, not how to establish such a permanent organization as the one contemplated, but how to rectify the constructional disequilibrium of the existing organization. For this purpose the most practical way was to find some kind of method for solving the difficulties of those currencies which served as the base of international finance, that is, the key currencies. This is the 'key countries (key currencies) approach', to which many subscribed, not only in the United States, but also in many other countries. As has already been stated in Chapter III, Section 3 and Chapter V, Section 2, such ideas were incorporated in the currency agreements of the 1930s and in Keynes's writings. The Clearing Union itself was merely the expression in a different form of the same idea. The existence of such a view is significant, if considered in relation to what is to follow, and so we shall examine it in some detail.

The American Bankers' Association, in its report published in September 1943, made a proposal to the following effect:

(a) Reform the Bank for International Settlements or set up an international organization in its place where international discussion on the stabilization of currency could take place.
(b) Credit should be granted only after a healthy economic plan had been set up.

(*c*) Credit should be granted in individual cases in accordance with fixed standards.

(*d*) Stabilize the dollar without any exchange restrictions and, then, establish a fixed rate between the dollar and the pound.

The above Association, in February 1945, urged the postponement of the operation of the 'Fund', and proposed that the 'Bank' should undertake the functions originally allocated to the 'Fund', which functions should be reinforced to enable it to grant loans for currency stabilization purposes. These views were very widely held in financial circles in the United States.

Leon Fraser, former Governor of the Bank for International Settlements, and Winthrop W. Aldrich, of the Chase National Bank, objected to both the 'Fund' and the 'Bank' and made proposals to the following effect:

Fraser proposed in November 1943 that (*a*) an agreement should be signed regarding the sterling-dollar exchange, (*b*) a gold credit to the extent of $5 billion should be granted to Britain, (*c*) the British liabilities resulting from the last war should be cancelled, (*d*) the repayment of debts contracted under the Lend Lease Act should be postponed for five years, and (*e*) the functions of the Bank for International Settlements should be expanded to cover mutual consultation and the granting of stabilization credits, and concluded that there was no need for a new international organization.

Then, Aldrich, in November 1944, urged that the following should be carried out to provide a solution of the key currencies: (*a*) settlement of the question of war debts between the United States and Britain, (*b*) reduction or abolition of all trade obstacles between the United States and the British Commonwealth, and (*c*) granting of assistance amounting to $3 billion to Britain under the above-mentioned conditions.

The leading advocate of this trend of thought was John H. Williams of Harvard.

He first made these views public in *Foreign Affairs* (January 1944 number). His arguments are given below:

The structural drawback of the IMF is that payments received for exports by the United States do not supplement the dollar holdings of the IMF, for that country does not need the currencies of other countries to pay for its imports. Therefore, even though the international balance of payments of the United States is maintained, the dollar funds of the IMF must be speedily dissipated. This is why provision should be made in the IMF Agreement for such a complicated matter as the repurchase of the currency of one's own country with gold or dollars and, at the same time, the United States should bear the whole responsibility of adjustment under the clauses of parity change and scarce currency. Moreover, under the expected post-war imbalance there is a danger of the above drawback being aggravated, against which the IMF is almost impotent. The initial steps, therefore, should be (*a*) first, to conclude an agreement concerning exchange rates, (*b*) then, to adjust them whenever necessary through international consultation, and (*c*) to expand the business of the 'Bank' and enable it to grant stabilization loans, since the 'Bank' is expected to play an important role even during the transitional period.[1]

The idea that if the dollar-sterling rate be stabilized in some way it could constitute the strong core of other stabilization plans had many supporters, J. H. Riddle and Gustav Cassel among them.[2]

However, Rasminsky, Director of the Foreign Exchange Control Board of Canada, submitted against this view that it was fraught with the danger of promoting economic regionalism and of dividing the world into several economic blocs.

Alvin Hansen stated that, as early as about 1941, he had already entertained the idea of Anglo-American co-operation on the three points of (*a*) parallel enforcement of economic expansion policies, (*b*) aid to less advanced countries for development purposes and (*c*) stabilization of the economy and the currency. Nevertheless he was soon convinced that such a plan operating between great countries would not obtain the co-operation of small countries and, further, that their interest would, after all, not be so well looked after as in the IMF Agreement. He thus made clear his pro-IMF attitude.[3] Morgenthau also stuck to his opinion that the 'key currencies

[1] John H. Williams, *Post-war Monetary Plans and other Essays*, p. 165.
[2] G. N. Halm, *International Monetary Co-operation*, p. 165.
[3] Alvin H. Hansen, *America's Role in the World Economy*, 1945, pp. 84-7.

approach' was 'a dictatorship of world finance by the two countries' and, as the Bretton Woods proposals were international they could only be put into practice through broad international co-operation.[1]

Ultimately, the 'key currencies approach' was forced to take second place to the universality of the IMF, and was only partially realized in the Anglo-American Financial Agreement of later days. In the post-war situation this has had the result that the U.S. dollar has acquired, not only complete leadership but also entire responsibility, and the role played by the pound has become of secondary importance, a mere adjunct to international liquidity.

Meantime, the opposition of the American conservatives to the IMF Agreement persisted tenaciously. For example, in spite of the fact that all representatives to the IMF should, as originally conceived, consist of neutral financial experts rather than government representatives, Congress demanded that they should be representatives approved by the Administration; should belong to the (U.S.) National Advisory Council on International Monetary and Financial Problems (set up under the Bretton Woods Agreements Act, Article IV) ; and, when required to vote in the Fund on any of the main clauses, should obtain this Council's approval.[2] Such a demand as this was entirely contrary to the British view that the granting of loans by the Fund should be automatic. In other fields, also, the views of the two countries differed widely.

In this situation even the clause concerning scarce currency could not in practice be enforced in respect of the U.S. dollars without the approval of the American Administration. Further-

[1] Richard N. Gardner, *Sterling-Dollar Diplomacy*, 1956, p. 138.
[2] According to the Bretton Woods Agreements Act, the representatives of the United States of America must obtain prior approval of the National Advisory Council in the event of their voting on the following matters :
(a) Relinquishment of the conditions for lending under Article V, Section 4 of the Agreement.
(b) Proclamation of U.S. dollar as scarce currency. (For (a) and (b), see Act, Article IV, (b) (4).) Next, without legislative approval of Congress, neither the President nor any one else may act for the United States in the following with respect to the Fund Agreement: (i) Demand or vote for a change of quotas. (Agreement Article III, Section 2.) (ii) Proposal of, agreement to, or approval of a uniform change in par values. (Agreement, Article IV, Sections 5 and 7; Article XX, Section 4.) (iii) Approval of the reform of the Agreement. (Article XVII.) (iv) Loans to the Fund. (For (a), (b), (c), and (d), see Act, Article V.)

more, according to the reply of the Administration in Congress, the primary object of the IMF was the stabilization of exchange rates and the orderly liberalization of exchange transactions, the granting of credit being only of secondary importance.

Not only that, but the rectification of an external imbalance required the taking of all possible measures to adjust the internal structure before resorting to a change of parity, which measure should be kept as a last resort.

While leaving several problems unsolved, the arguments in the United States petered out toward the middle of July 1945. Although in the Senate efforts were still being made to postpone approval, the Bretton Woods Agreements were nevertheless passed on 18 July 1945, some months earlier than in Britain.

Thus the Bretton Woods organization, which had been under violent discussion since the publication of the drafts of the two agreements, was duly constituted in December 1945 by the signatures of the representatives of 35 countries. In March in the following year the United States, in accordance with the regulations, convoked the first annual meeting of the Board of Governors (inaugural meeting) at Savannah, Georgia. This is generally called the Savannah Conference.

At this conference much bargaining took place. For example, discussion took place as to where the headquarters of the two organizations should be situated: this, though seemingly unimportant, was not necessarily so. The British were of the opinion that they should be located in New York, their reason being that they thought that the organizations would be less susceptible to political influences in New York than in Washington. This argument was connected with their insistence that the delegates should be international financial experts free of all political colour.

The Americans, however, insisted upon Washington as headquarters.

The object of this was the intention of the Treasury-White Group, to exclude the influence of Wall Street and to increase political control. In accordance with their wishes, it was decided that the seat should be at Washington, exposed to Congressional influence. Moreover, at about that time Morgenthau was replaced by Vinson, and relations between the United States and the Soviet Union became more strained than ever before, resulting in noticeably increased pressure by the nationalists.

In this way, the operations of the two organizations became subject to the influences of many national interests, especially of the United States, with the result that their international character was thereby diminished. Thus the newly-born 'hybrids', as Keynes called them, were neither as strong nor as true to their objective as he had hoped.

Eventually, the 'Bank' commenced operations on 25 June 1946, and the 'Fund' in March 1947, and they have remained in operation to this day.

In the following chapters the main clauses of the 'Fund' will be explained and an examination made of the function and working of the IMF system.

VI

FUNCTION AND ORGANIZATION OF THE INTERNATIONAL MONETARY FUND

Section 1.—Member Countries and their Subscriptions

1. Member Countries

THE IMF consists of its original members and others (Article II). There is no substantial difference in the qualifications for membership of the above two groups, but the procedure at the time of their entry is different. The former are those countries which participated in the Bretton Woods Conference, completed ratification by the end of 1946 (under the original Agreement, the deadline was the end of 1945, but at the Savannah inaugural meeting a decision was taken to extend the date by one year), and deposited their advice of agreement with the American Administration. The original members were 39 in all, that is, the 44 allied countries which were present at the above Conference less Australia, Haiti, Liberia, New Zealand and the Soviet Union. (Australia, Haiti and Liberia, however, later joined the Fund.) The other members were those countries which later became members in accordance with the terms prescribed by the IMF. The actual procedure was for such countries to request participation and present their requests to the Board of Governors (to be touched upon later) and, for the Executive Directors then to decide upon the conditions (such as quotas and methods of payments) which were then to be approved by the Board of Governors, and, lastly, the petitioning countries signed the Agreement and deposited their advice of agreement with the American Administration. The total of other members was 39 as at the end of May 1962. According to Article XX, Section 2 of the Agreement, 'By their signing of this Agreement, all Governments accept it both on their own behalf and in respect of all their colonies, overseas territories, all territories under their protection, suzerainty, or authority and all territories in respect of which they exercise a mandate', and so the Agreement covers not only their homelands but also all the areas under their control.

If a member wishes to withdraw from the Fund, it is always possible for it to do so by advising the IMF authorities to that effect, and the withdrawal becomes effective as from the date the notice has been received (Article XV, Section 1). On 14 March 1953, Poland, one of the original members, exercised its right of withdrawal, giving as a reason that the IMF was a mere puppet of the United States Government. Besides a voluntary withdrawal, a member may be asked to withdraw from the IMF. Thus, should a member fail to fulfil one or other of its obligations under the Agreement, the Fund may declare the member ineligible to make use of the resources of the Fund. If, after the expiration of a reasonable period the member persists in its failure to fulfil one or other of its obligations, it may be required to relinquish its membership of the Fund by a decision of the Board of Governors (Article XV, Section 2). On 31 December 1954, Czechoslovakia, an original member, was, in accordance with this rule, expelled from the Fund.

Thus, at the end of May 1962, the total membership of the IMF stood at 76, of which, 37 were original members, which means that, with the exception of the Communist countries and Switzerland, all the leading countries of the world had joined the Fund.

It may be remembered that participation in the International Bank for Reconstruction and Development, which was also established by the Bretton Woods Agreements, is permitted only if the country concerned is a member of the IMF, but participation in the IMF is possible without joining the International Bank for Reconstruction and Development. Therefore, though Cuba and Dominica withdrew from the International Bank for Reconstruction and Development on 4 November 1960 and on 1 December 1960, respectively, they were able to retain their IMF membership.

2. Quotas

Member countries are required to subscribe a certain sum to the IMF as a joint exchange fund for the purpose of achieving the Fund's objectives. The initial subscriptions were scheduled to total $11,000 million of which $8,800 million was to be subscribed by the original members and the balance by the other members. These subscriptions were made on the basis of quotas fixed for the members, and their quotas are set forth in Schedule A attached to the Agreement for the original members and fixed by the IMF when any other country joined the Fund. These quotas, as will be explained later, greatly influence the positions and rights of members in that they serve as the basis for the use of the resources of the Fund and as a standard for the voting rights in the Fund. This is the reason why there was a great difference between the methods of deciding quotas of the White and the Keynes Plans owing to the divergence of British and American interests. In the White Plan, it was provided that the quotas should be fixed on the basis of gold holdings, of the fluctuations and scale of international balances of payments, and of national incomes, while in the Keynes Plan it was provided that they should be fixed on the basis of the average exports and imports for the three pre-war years. In the IMF Agreement, a firm basis for calculation is not clearly provided, but on the whole, it is in accord with the White Plan, in that they were to be calculated on the basis of monetary reserves, volume of foreign trade, and national income of each member, and, in addition, political considerations were to some extent taken into account.

3. Change in Quotas

The quotas thus fixed are not unchangeable, although they cannot be adjusted automatically according to changes in circumstances. The IMF will, however, consider the adjustment of a member's quota, if requested to do so. The quotas of small members have, in fact, often been changed. Again, the IMF will every five years review the quotas of its members and, if it thinks fit, propose their adjustment. Such changes, however, require not less than a four-fifths majority of the total voting power and the consent of the member countries concerned (Article III, Section 2).

In accordance with these provisions, the IMF Executive Directors set up a special committee in December 1954 to make a wholesale review of existing quotas. The resolution of the Executive Directors at that time was (1) that consideration should be given to a case-by-case increase in the quotas of small-quota members, but (2) that no wholesale adjustment of the quotas should then be carried out (this resolution was adopted on 19 January 1956). However, at the time of the Suez Crisis, there was an active demand for IMF funds and the shortage of these funds was keenly felt. At the same time, voices were raised, with good reason, pointing out that the quotas had been left at the same level as when the Fund was instituted, although ten years had elapsed and world trade had doubled in volume, while the foreign exchange reserves of its members had increased by 50 per cent. Under these circumstances, when the annual meeting of the Board of Governors was held at New Delhi in October 1958, the representative of the United States of America proposed that the Executive Directors should consider an increase of the quotas; his proposal was adopted unanimously, the Executive Directors resolving that:

1. The quotas of the members as at 31 January 1959 should be increased uniformly by 50 per cent, but
2. Those members whose quotas were small (not more than $15 million) should, if they wished, be permitted to increase their quotas by not more than 50 per cent in accordance with the principle of adjustment of small quotas, and
3. Canada, West Germany and Japan should be permitted to increase their quotas by more than 50 per cent, in view of their position in world trade, and their recent relative economic growth:

> Canada (uniform 50 per cent increase would have been $450 million) — $550 million;
> West Germany (uniform 50 per cent increase would have been $495 million) — $787.5 million;
> Japan (uniform 50 per cent increase would have been $375 million) — $500 million.

The increases proposed by the Executive Directors were formally agreed to and approved by the Governors of the member countries on 2 February 1959. Thus, the total quotas of the IMF rose from $9,193 million at the end of 1958 to $15,056 million at the end of May 1962.

4. Method of Payment of the Quotas

As mentioned above a member pays its subscription according to the quota fixed at the time of entry. The form of such payment is as follows:

Each member shall pay in gold, as a minimum, the smaller of

(1) 25 per cent of its quota; or
(2) 10 per cent of its net official holdings of gold and U.S. dollars

at the date when the Fund notifies members that it will shortly be in a position to begin exchange transactions. The balance is to be paid in its own currency (Article III, Section 3). The same principle also applies to the above-mentioned increase in the quota, 25 per cent of the increased amount being payable in gold and the balance in its own currency (Article III, Section 4). The payment should be made when joining the Fund, on or before the date when the member becomes eligible to buy currencies from the Fund, following the fixing of its parity, and, in the case of an increase of its quota, within thirty days after the date of its consent to such an increase. Should any country, in the case of an increase in its quota, meet difficulty in making payment immediately, it is provided that gold should be held at the depositories designated by that member which has the largest quota (Article XIII). At present, the New York Federal Reserve Bank, the Bank of England, the Bank of France and the Reserve Bank of India are designated as such depositories. As far as the currencies of the member countries are concerned, their central banks should credit the account of the IMF with them as holders for the IMF (Article XIII, Section 2). If, however, the IMF does not require the currency of any member for its operations, that member may be permitted to substitute non-negotiable, non-interest bearing notes on demand or similar obligations issued by that member or by its central bank and held by it for account of the IMF.

Section 2.—Establishment and Alteration
of Par Values

In view of the experience of exchange devaluation in the
1930s, which brought confusion to international exchange
transactions, the stabilization of exchange rates following the
introduction of the White Plan was the most important consideration in the drafting of the IMF Agreement.

It was recognized that efforts should be made to establish a
connection with gold and to break the rigidity of an unchangeable gold parity.

In the IMF Agreement, therefore, the system adopted
permits the members on the one hand to set up their own
managed currency systems and, on the other, it imposes
restrictions upon their freedom of altering the external value
of their currencies, which thus places them under the control
of an international organization. Under the IMF Agreement,
therefore, the currencies of all members are attached to gold
as the common denominator, and any alteration of external
values in later years must not, in principle, be made without
the concurrence of the IMF. That part of the Agreement
which relates to this matter is dealt with below.

1. Establishment of Par Values

Member countries accept the obligations to fix the par
values of their currencies in co-operation with the IMF. These
par values should be expressed in terms of gold or in terms of
the U.S. dollar of the weight and fineness as at 1 July 1944
($35 per ounce of fine gold) (Article IV, Section 1). This
means that under the International Monetary Fund system,
the par value is directly attached to gold, and, since there is
no special international currency unit such as Bancor, which
had been proposed by the Keynes Plan, the position of gold as
a world currency has been firmly established and maintained.

The biggest problem to be tackled following the inaugura-
tion of the IMF was the choice of initial par values for members'
currencies. The procedure was as follows:

1. When the Fund was of the opinion that it would shortly
   be in a position to begin exchange transactions (practically,

as will be stated later, to make loans to the member countries of the IMF), it would so notify the members and
request them to communicate within thirty days the par
values of their currencies based on the rates of exchange
prevailing on the sixtieth day before the entry into force of
this Agreement.

2. If no objection is raised by either the IMF or the member
countries concerned to the par values communicated, they
would be adopted as the initial par values. If there be any
objection, then both parties should agree upon suitable par
values within a period determined by the Fund. If the
Fund and the members concerned cannot agree within
that period, then these member countries are considered as
having withdrawn from the Fund.

3. After the par values have been determined in this way, the
members concerned are then in a position to buy foreign
currencies from the Fund.

In accordance with the above regulations, on 12 September
1946, the IMF requested members to communicate their par
values based upon the exchange rates ruling on 28 October 1945.
In consequence, the initial par values of 32 of the original
members were established on 18 December 1946. Seven
asked for postponement.[1]

Once having fixed their par values, members accepted the
following clear obligations in order to maintain their parities
and to ensure their effectiveness.

In the event of members buying or selling gold, they should
not buy at a price above par value plus the margin prescribed
by the IMF or sell at a price below par value less the prescribed
margin (Article IV, Section 2). The margin, according to the
Articles of Agreement, should be one of the following:

1. One-quarter of 1 per cent plus the following charges:
   (a) The actual or computed cost of converting the gold
   transferred into gold delivery bars at the normal centre
   for dealing in gold of either the buying member or the
   member whose currency is exchanged for the gold;
   (b) The actual or computed cost of transporting the gold

---

[1] The original members requesting postponement of their initial par values
were Brazil, China, Dominica, Greece, Poland, Uruguay and Yugoslavia.

transferred to the normal centre for dealing in gold of either the buying member or the member whose currency is exchanged for the gold;

(*c*) Any charges made by the custodian of the gold transferred for effecting the transfer; or

2. 1 per cent which 1 per cent shall be taken to include all of the charges set forth in 1 above.

The maximum and the minimum rates for exchange transactions between the currencies of members shall not differ from parity.

1. For spot exchange transactions, by more than 1 per cent; and

2. for other exchange transactions, by a margin which exceeds the margin for spot exchange transactions by more than the Fund considers reasonable.

In order to fulfil the above obligations, members are requested to take such appropriate measures as will ensure that those exchange transactions which are conducted between their own currencies and other members' currencies in their own territories will be carried out at those exchange rates which are within the above limits (for example, that the currency authorities should fix the buying and selling rates within 1 per cent above or below their parities and, at these rates, effect without limit the purchase and sale of foreign currencies with exchange banks). If, however, like the United States of America of today, the monetary authorities freely buy and sell gold within the above-mentioned limits, then this should be regarded as fulfilling the obligation concerning exchange rates margins.[1]

In addition to the above, a member is required to collaborate with the Fund to promote exchange stability, to maintain orderly exchange dealings with other members, and to avoid competitive parity changes.

The restoration of external convertibility of the West European countries' currencies toward the end of 1958, broadened the interpretation of the regulations concerning exchange rate margins. By the restoration of the external

[1] At present U.S. are buying from and selling to foreign monetary authorities or central banks only.

convertibility of their currencies, the OEEC countries brought into effect the European Monetary Agreement (EMA). The OEEC countries took measures to maintain their currencies within the limit of 1 per cent above and below par value prescribed by the IMF, but, at the same time, these rates were subjected to arbitrage dealings on the market. Therefore, even if the OEEC countries maintain their basic rates against the U.S. dollar within 1 per cent of their parities (as a matter of fact 0·75 per cent in many countries), rates may none the less go beyond the limits prescribed by the IMF, for should the dollar rate move to 1 per cent above its parity on one market while on another it is 1 per cent below its parity, the difference above and below parity would be approximately 2 per cent. Such being the case, the IMF, recognizing the contribution the foreign exchange markets in the OEEC countries make towards the maintenance of convertibility, made the following decision on July 1959: 'The Fund does not object to exchange rates which are within 2 per cent of parity for spot transactions between one member's currency and the currencies of other members, when the basic rate is within the margin of 1 per cent'.

2. Change in Par Values

The main characteristic of the IMF Agreement is that while stabilizing the exchange rates of its members by the obligation to establish par values, it permits a change under certain conditions. Thus the system is not as rigid as the gold standard system. What, then, are the conditions for a change in par values? The principles are two:

1. A member can propose a change in the par value of its own currency only when it is necessary to correct a fundamental disequilibrium.
2. A change in the par value of a member's currency may be made only on the proposal of the member concerned and only after consultation with the Fund.

Though a member may be permitted to change the par value of its own currency when it is necessary to rectify a fundamental disequilibrium, the IMF Agreement has not rigidly defined the meaning of fundamental disequilibrium, and it is left therefore entirely to the Fund's own judgment. The reason for this is that it is difficult to define clearly beforehand the phenomenon of fundamental disequilibrium, and, further, that, if a rigid definition were given in the Agreement, the IMF would be prevented from adopting an elastic policy in the treatment of subsequent cases. It was natural, therefore, that active discussions should take place on the interpretation of fundamental disequilibrium. We shall give one example to make clear its connection with the operation of the Agreement. Suppose that a member, owing to its commodity prices being higher than international prices, has developed an adverse balance of payments. The fundamental measures that could be taken by this member in order to achieve a balance between internal and external prices, seem to be two : (1) to reduce its commodity prices to the international level; or (2) to devalue. Under the gold standard system, however, the member concerned would have had to resort to the former measure, and so become subject to the evil of deflation ; this sacrifice of the internal economy was the gravest drawback of that system. In the IMF Agreement, however, the existence of a fundamental disequilibrium in such a case is taken for granted, and approval may be given for its correction by a measure of devaluation. In connection with the interpretation of fundamental disequilibrium, the British Government asked the IMF authorities in September 1946, whether, in the event of any member suffering from chronic or persistent unemployment, due to pressure on its balance of payments, and finding it necessary to resort to measures designed to protect its economy, it is possible to say that there exists a fundamental disequilibrium in that country? The IMF, as we may suppose, acknowledging the validity of the questions, adopted a resolution recognizing the existence under the circumstances of a fundamental disequilibrium. Even if there is a fundamental disequilibrium, the change in par value can be made only on the proposal of the member concerned and only after consultation with the Fund. The attitude of the IMF toward a change in par value is therefore wholly passive in that, even when there clearly exists a fundamental disequilibrium, the proposal of the member concerned precedes the change in par value, and the IMF does not take the initiative in proposing the change.

Should a member desire to make a change in the par value of its currency, it should present its proposal together with a statement that it is necessary for the purpose of correcting a fundamental disequilibrium. If the proposed change, (*a*) with all previous changes, (*b*) whether increases or decreases,

(1) does not exceed 10 per cent of the initial par value, the IMF would raise no objection;
(2) does not exceed a further 10 per cent of the initial par value, the IMF may either concur or object, but must declare its attitude within seventy-two hours if the member so requests;
(3) is not within (1) or (2), the IMF may either concur or object, but would be entitled to a longer period in which to declare its attitude.[1]

(Article IV, Section 5, C)

Thus, the change in a par value that can be carried out at the discretion of the member concerned, is, as a matter of fact, limited to 10 per cent or less of the initial par value, and a change of a greater extent requires the prior approval of the IMF. On the other hand, the IMF, if it is satisfied that the change is necessary to correct a fundamental disequilibrium would always concur in the proposed change and would raise no objection, whatever the domestic, social, or political policies of the member may be (Article IV, Section 5, (*f*)).

A change in par value is thus subjected to fairly rigid regulations. If a member changes its par value in spite of the objection of the IMF, it should, in principle, be debarred from using the resources of the IMF, and if, after the expiration of a reasonable period, the dispute between the member and the IMF continues, it may be required to withdraw from membership of the IMF by a ruling of the Board of Governors (Article

---

[1] The comparison of the regulations of the IMF with those of the Keynes Plan, concerning changes in par values shows that there are two differences: first, while the Keynes Plan restricted the discretion of a member to change the par value of its currency to 5 per cent and, moreover, gave it only to permanent debtor countries, the IMF Agreement raised the discretionary range to 10 per cent and gave it to all members, whether debtor or creditor; and, further, while the Keynes Plan provided that the Union should advise a member to adjust its exchange and made its agreement to the change a condition for being able to draw on the Union, the IMF Agreement stipulated that the IMF authorities should not propose any exchange adjustment, and a change in par value should not be a pre-condition before funds were available (see Chapter V, Section 4).

IV, Section 6, and Article XV, Section 2). Czechoslovakia was an example of this compulsory withdrawal when, in June 1953, it carried out a currency reform and devalued its par value from 5.0 koruna per dollar to 7.20 koruna without consulting the IMF. Though the IMF sought the reasons for this change, Czechoslovakia did not reply. The Executive Directors, therefore, declared on 4 November 1953 that this member was no longer eligible to use IMF funds. As there was no reply, Czechoslovakia's name was struck off the roll of members on 31 December 1954.

In this connection, it may not be amiss to add that, although a change in par value requires the satisfaction of the two general conditions mentioned above, the Agreement makes provision for two exceptional cases. One is that if the change does not affect the international transactions of the members, a member may change the par value of its currency without its concurrence (Article IV, Section 5, (e)). The other, which is of greater practical importance, concerns the uniform changes in par values provided for in Article IV, Section 7.

3. Uniform Changes in Par Values

As has already been stated, the change in the par value of the currency of a member should, in principle, be made on the proposal of that member, but Article IV, Section 7 provides that

(1) by a majority of the total voting power and
(2) when approved by every member having 10 per cent or more of the total quotas of the IMF (in practice, the United States of America and Britain),

the par values of the currencies of all members can be freely uniformly and automatically changed. However, even if such uniform changes take place, any member not wishing the par value of its currency to be changed, may be granted exemption, if, within seventy-two hours of the change, the IMF is advised to that effect.

These changes in par values, as a rule, change the par values of the currencies of all the members at the same time at the same rate, and so the relations among these currencies do not undergo any change. The insertion of this clause was made, however, with the intention of correcting the gravest drawback of the gold standard system, under which the stability of commodity prices is universally threatened by a shortage or surplus of gold. As the currencies of all members had thereby been rigidly linked to gold, variations in gold production affected the supply of currency and consequently the level of commodity prices throughout the world. It follows therefore, that when gold production is relatively high, thus raising the prices of commodities, it is imperative to remedy this by a uniform increase in the gold par values of all currencies. Conversely, when gold production is low and some action is required to check the decline of world commodity prices, this would take the form of reducing all par values. However, as all currencies are assuming more and more the character of managed currencies, the role of gold as a reserve for currency has gradually become less important. Thus, gold today serves rather as a reserve for external settlement than as a domestic reserve. This being the case, the problem today is not so much the effect that gold output may have on world prices as whether it can provide sufficient reserves for universal external settlements to cope with growing international trade. This leads us to discuss uniform changes in par values, as an adequate solution of the problems of international liquidity.

4. Changes in Par Value and Maintenance of the Gold Value of IMF's Assets

Lastly, the value of the assets held by the IMF must be maintained on the basis of gold (Article IV, Section 8). Should the foreign exchange value of a member's currency be considered to have depreciated to a significant extent, the member is required to pay to the IMF within a reasonable time the amount of its own currency equal to the decline in the gold value of the currency held by the IMF and, conversely, when the par value of a member's currency has increased, the IMF must return to the member within a reasonable time an amount equal to the increase in the gold value. These provisions apply to a uniform proportionate change in the par values of the currencies of all the members, unless, at the time when such a change is proposed, the IMF decides otherwise.

Section 3.—Abolition of Exchange Restrictions

In view of the bitter experience in the 1930s of restricted and distorted world trade brought about by the disorder in the international exchanges, the IMF Agreement has, as one of its aims, the establishment of a free, stable, multilateral and non-discriminatory system for international payments. It is quite natural, therefore, that the Agreement should have laid stress upon the avoidance of the disorderly devaluations and restrictions upon the healthy development of international trade that were universal during the 1930s. Article VIII embodies this principle and imposes upon its members in effect the following three obligations regarding the abolition of exchange restrictions :

1. Avoidance of restrictions upon current payments.
2. Avoidance of discriminatory currency practices.
3. Convertibility of foreign-held balances.

1. Avoidance of Restrictions upon Current Payments

Members should not impose restrictions upon payments for current international transactions. This means that a resident in a member country may at any time exchange the currency of his own country for such foreign currency as is necessary for external payments.

This regulation may be interpreted as an obligation to maintain the convertibility of a resident current account.

By payments for current transactions is meant those payments which are not, in fact, transfers of capital. The Agreement gives the following examples of payments covered by this definition :

1. All payments due in connection with foreign trade, other current business, including services, and normal short-term banking and credit facilities.
2. Payments due as interest on loans and as net income from other investments.
3. Payments of a moderate amount for amortization of loans or for depreciation of direct investments.
4. Moderate remittances for family living expenses.

The current transactions covered by the Agreement are not necessarily limited to the above items, but in case of doubt as to whether given transactions are to be regarded as capital or current transactions, the IMF would decide in consultation with the members concerned.

In the IMF Agreement, the basic principle of the abolition of exchange restrictions applies exclusively to current transactions, since there is no regulation whatsoever regarding exchange restrictions on the movement of capital, the matter being entirely at the discretion of the members concerned. Not only that, but, should a member make use of IMF funds for capital movements, the IMF could request the member concerned to enforce appropriate measures of control. Such an attitude by the IMF is quite understandable when we recall the movement of hot money and other capital in the period between the two World Wars, which were tremendously disturbing factors in international finance. Technically, however, it is very difficult to regulate capital transactions strictly, while current exchange transactions are left entirely free. For example, when foreign currency needed for foreign travel can be obtained quite freely, there is inevitably a risk that there should be an outflow of capital on that pretext. This did not constitute a serious problem during the post-war transitional period (to be touched upon later), when exchange control was allowed in those exceptional circumstances, but today, when the restrictions upon current exchange transactions have been removed to a great extent, control over capital transactions would appear to be very difficult to achieve in practice. However, in spite of such technical difficulties, a new formula for the control of capital transactions is being developed in certain countries in these post-war days. For instance, some South American countries, such as Brazil and Peru, and some others, Belgium being one of them, have divided the post-war exchange market into two parts, one for current and the other for capital transactions.

They strictly observe the margins on exchange rates fixed by the IMF Agreement in the former, and in the latter leave the exchange rates to fluctuate freely in all transactions officially permitted. This *modus operandi* of leaving capital transactions to be adjusted freely through fluctuations in exchange rates, instead of resorting to direct control, is also found in the regulations for the liberalization of capital transactions in the European Common Market. These regulations, while adhering to the basic principle of the liberalization of capital transactions within the area of the Common Market, do not necessarily require the application of official rates only.

The provisions concerning current transactions in the IMF Agreement, as is mentioned above, concern payments or transfers, and do not prohibit restrictions upon current transactions themselves. However, as exchange restrictions can easily be replaced by trade control, the intentions of the IMF Agreement can be weakened, if import control measures take the place of those exchange restrictions which have been abolished in accordance with the Agreement. This is one of the reasons why close co-operation is maintained between IMF and GATT. Moreover, one of GATT's basic principles is that participating countries should not resort to import control for difficulties in their international balance of payments, unless the IMF considers that such difficulties do exist.

2. Avoidance of Discriminatory Currency Practices

While ensuring as much as possible the liberalization of current exchange transactions, the IMF Agreement requires members to avoid discriminatory currency practices that distort international trade. These are arrangements that specifically define the settlement terms applying to contracts exclusively between the countries concerned, as in the cases of bilateral agreements, barter transactions, the export and import link system, the retention of exchange quota systems, and the like. The multiple exchange rate system, which applies different rates to different transactions, according to their nature or class of goods, also belongs to this category, and its application is also prohibited unless approved by the IMF.

3. Convertibility of Foreign-held Balances

There is also the obligation to establish a multilateral settlement system. Under this members are required to maintain the convertibility of foreign-held balances of its own currency — in other words — convertibility of a non-resident account. Members must undertake to convert their own currency balances held by other members into the currencies of those members at their request or to settle in gold. Countries in the following circumstances, however, are exempted :

1. Where a member restricts the convertibility of its own currency by exchange control measures during the post-war transitional period, or controls the movement of capital.
2. Where balances held by another member, accumulated as a result of transactions effected during the post-war transitional period when restrictions were in force.
3. Where balances are held by another member and acquired in violation of the exchange control regulations of that member to which a request for conversion is made.
4. Where the currency of the member making the request for conversion has been declared a scarce currency (to be touched upon later).
5. Where a member to which a request for conversion is made is barred for some reason from using the resources of the IMF.

In all other cases, as had already been stated, members are obliged to permit convertibility into other currencies or in gold ; but according to the IMF Agreement, this obligation is governed by the following conditions :

1. proof is required that the balances to be converted have been recently acquired as a result of current transactions ; or
2. that their conversion is required for making payments for current transactions.

It is very doubtful whether, in practice, such proof is possible, for it is rather as a result of intervention in their own exchange market than as a result of individual transactions that the central bank of a member acquires the currency of another member. For example, if we assume that the balance of payments of a member shows a surplus of receipts over payments, then its foreign exchange market will have a surplus of foreign currencies ; these are then sold to its central bank by the banks dealing in foreign exchange. However, the central bank does not usually enquire as to whether these foreign currencies were acquired through current transactions and is therefore incapable of proving whether they have been or not. In consequence, the existing IMF Agreement ruling on this matter is countered by the fact that the convertibility of a currency is assured only so long as the member that has issued the currency has the intention of maintaining it. The rule under review is therefore of very doubtful value.

4. Exceptions to the Rules for the Avoidance of Various Restrictions upon the Foreign Exchanges

We have seen that a member is, in principle, under the obligation to remove all restrictions on current exchange transactions, and it is appropriate to mention here that a member which has accepted the three obligations mentioned on page 110 and is discharging them, is called an Article VIII country. The IMF Agreement has, however, laid down the following two exceptions to the rules.

First, where the IMF has declared a particular currency to be scarce (as to which details will be given later); here we may note that when the currency of a member has become scarce, the IMF authorities will advise other members to that effect. In consequence, members may exercise the right of imposing discriminatory restrictions upon exchange transactions in that particular currency, instead of restrictions being imposed upon the use of IMF funds with respect to that particular currency (Article VII).

Second, the post-war transitional period mentioned in Article XIV in the Agreement. This Article provides that members, by giving notice to the IMF, may maintain and adapt to changing circumstances their restrictions upon current exchange transactions during such transitional period as is necessary for reconstruction following the Second World War; as is well known, many members applied some measure of exchange control after the war on the basis of this rule. Incidentally, such members are generally called Article XIV countries as opposed to Article VIII countries. This transitional period was expected to end in 1952, that is, five years after the IMF commenced operations, and those members which subsequently maintained their restrictive measures were obliged to consult the IMF about their cancellation. Those consultations have been held by the IMF with the Article XIV countries every year since 1952.

At the end of 1960, contrary to initial expectations, only 10 members in the Americas had accepted Article VIII, these being Canada, Cuba, Dominica, El Salvador, Guatemala, Haiti, Honduras, Mexico, Panama and the United States. (Venezuela, though it has not formally notified the IMF of its agreement, is nevertheless regarded by the IMF as having done so.)

The improvement in the economics of the West European countries since 1955 gradually opened the door to a movement towards Article VIII country status. Thus, in February 1961 Britain, the Common Market countries and others, numbering 11 in all, became Article VIII countries.[1] In this way, sixteen years after the signing of its Agreement, the IMF is at long last approaching a state of affairs in matters of exchange control for which it had been planned.

Section 4.—Measures to Adjust Temporary Disequilibrium in the Balance of Payments

1. General Characteristics

The international monetary system under the IMF is designed to ensure the stability of exchange rates and the freedom of exchange transactions by international agreement. Whilst its basic function is the stabilization of exchange rates, it nevertheless permits changes in par values whenever there exists a 'fundamental disequilibrium'. At the same time, it offers an important defence against a short-term disequilibrium, in its facilities for the supply of foreign exchange. All members may use IMF resources under certain conditions when there is disequilibrium in international payments.

This idea arose from the intention of making countries with export surpluses provide funds to those with import surpluses to meet the latter's temporary shortages. This could be done through an international organization to be established by mutual co-operation between countries for the purpose of eliminating the drawback of the gold standard system, *i.e.* the

---

[1] The six member countries of the European Economic Community (West Germany, France, Italy, the Netherlands, Belgium and Luxemburg), Britain and Sweden (two of the EFTA countries), Eire and Peru formally became Article VIII countries on 15 February 1961 and Saudi Arabia on 23 February 1961.

painful deflation that a temporary deficit in international payments inflicts upon a country. The inspiration of the IMF, therefore, does not differ from that of the Keynes Plan, but there is a great difference in respect of its mechanism. The first point of difference concerns the method of raising the necessary financial resources. While the financial resources of the IMF commence with the joint subscriptions paid by its members in proportion to their quotas, the Keynes Plan needs no such prior subscriptions, as each member automatically makes an advance out of its excess of exports over imports up to the limit of its quota. In other words, the IMF has adopted a so-called deposit system while that of the Keynes Plan is an overdraft system. Second, in the Keynes Plan for an International Clearing Union, there are functional connections between the supply of funds and multilateral settlement, whereas in the IMF no such relation exists. A country in temporary disequilibrium should first make use of its exchange reserves, and only when these are running short should dependence be placed on advances from outside. In order to achieve a smooth international monetary system, therefore, it is necessary to establish an organization which will permit the exchange reserves of member countries to be freely mobilized so that their international imbalance of payments may be adjusted. It may also be necessary to prepare appropriate measures to meet the possibility that a country may not be able to mobilize its export earnings in one country to compensate for its excess of imports from another. In this connection, in the Keynes Plan the greater part of members' international transactions is concentrated in an internal organization, where their respective credits and debits are set off multilaterally and their final balances are adjusted through that organization. The IMF, however, does not have this function; instead, it seeks to achieve multilateral compensation by requiring each member, under Article VIII, Section 4 of the Agreement, to maintain the convertibility of any balances in its own currency that may be held by another member.

2. Mechanism for Supply of Funds

The plan is that the supply of funds provided by the IMF should be handed over only to the official agency designated by the member concerned, such as its treasury, central bank, stabilization fund (Article V, Section 1). In consequence, there is no question of the IMF supplying funds directly to exchange banks in the member's country. This does not, however, constitute any great impediment to the IMF's objective of relieving a member of its short-term international payments difficulties. For example, when a member develops an import surplus, a shortage of foreign currency appears in its foreign exchange market, but the banks conducting foreign exchange business usually turn to the authorities to make good this deficiency. As a result, the unfavourable balance of international payments is reflected in a fall in official exchange reserves; if the authorities can obtain foreign currency from the IMF, then they can help to correct the unfavourable balance.

The supply of funds by the IMF in this matter is a species of lending. The term 'lending' does not appear in the Agreement at all, the phrase 'exchange transaction' between the member and IMF being used instead; this is because the acquisition by a member of a foreign currency from the IMF takes the form of a purchase in exchange for its own currency. For example, a member that wishes to acquire U.S. dollars pays its currency to the IMF, and in exchange receives the U.S. dollars; this is certainly nothing but an exchange transaction. The exchange rates in these cases are based, needless to say, upon the exchange parities previously established by the members.[1]

Though the supply of foreign currency by the IMF to a member is usually conducted in the above-mentioned way, any member desiring to obtain the currency of another member for gold must sell gold to the IMF, if it can do so with equal advantage (Article V, Section 6 (*a*)). But a member is exempted from this obligation to sell gold to the IMF when the gold is newly produced from mines located within its territories (Article V, Section 6 (*b*)).

[1] The IMF permitted Belgium, Canada and some others to adopt the floating-rate system, and exchange transactions between these countries and the Fund were based upon the average dollar rate of their own currencies in their exchange markets at the time of a transaction. Further, the IMF holdings of their currencies are periodically adjusted to the changes in their currencies so as to maintain their gold values.

3. Restricting Regulations for Supply of Funds

Although funds are made available in the manner described above, their supply is subject to certain limitations. Apart from those relating to payment in gold, these include the following :

(a) *Restrictions upon use of Foreign Currency*

First, the foreign currencies supplied by the IMF are generally intended for current transactions. A member may not therefore use IMF funds for other purposes such as, for example, relief or reconstruction, settlement of international indebtedness or reparations arising from previous capital indebtedness. Moreover these should be genuine current payments and a member is not entitled without the IMF's permission to use its resources to acquire currency to hold against exchange transactions. Further, when it desires to purchase another member's currency, it should affirm that it is in fact needed for making current payments in that currency (Article V, Section 3).

Though the supply of funds by the IMF is usually limited to payments for current transactions, the Agreement has exceptionally provided that the use of IMF funds is permitted for capital movement purposes in the following two cases only :

1. When they are required for capital transactions of a reasonable amount, for the expansion of exports or for the ordinary course of trade, banking or business (Article VI, Section 1) ; or

2. When they are needed for capital transfers by a member, the IMF's holdings of whose currency have remained below 75 per cent of its quota for an immediately preceding period of not less than six months. Even in this case, however, purchases of foreign currencies for capital transfers are not permitted if they have the effect of raising the IMF's holdings of the currency of the member concerned above 75 per cent of its quota, or of reducing the IMF's holdings of the currency desired below 75 per cent of the quota of the member whose currency is desired (Article VI, Section 2).

(b) *Restrictions due to Scarcity of Currencies held by the IMF*

The use of IMF funds is restricted by the amounts of member's currencies held by the IMF. For instance, in the event of the currency of a member held by the IMF becoming scarce as a result of an active demand for it and the IMF declaring it to be a scarce currency, restriction in the use of IMF funds so far as that currency is concerned would be imposed upon every member. We shall later touch upon the declaration of a scarce currency.

(c) *Restrictions upon Amounts based upon Quotas*

Another important restriction is that the sum of IMF funds to be used by a member is limited by the amount of its fixed quota. The Agreement stipulates the extent that IMF funds may be used by each member as follows (Article V, Section 3, (*a*) (iii)) :

1. The proposed purchase should not cause the Fund's holdings of the purchasing member's currency to increase by more than 25 per cent of its quota during the period of one year ending on the date of the purchase. So long as the IMF's holding of the currency of that member does not exceed 75 per cent of its quota, the member is exempt from the above restriction until it reaches 75 per cent of its quota.
2. The Fund's holding of the purchasing member's currency must not exceed 200 per cent of the quota of that member.

The maximum limit for a member wishing to receive a supply of funds from the IMF in exchange for its own currency is reached, therefore, when the IMF's holding of its currency reaches double the amount of that country's quota ; but, as each member has already paid in its own currency 75 per cent of its quota as its subscription to the IMF, the limit for raising foreign currencies is, as a matter of fact, 125 per cent of its quota. A member is only exceptionally permitted to make use of IMF funds to this limit at one and the same time, but the basic principle is that this 25 per cent of its quota may be used for one year. When a purchase of its currency is made by some other member, then the member concerned is released from the above-mentioned limit of 25 per cent and the limit is increased by the extent of the purchase of its currency ; the full 25 per cent applies otherwise.

(d) *Relaxation of Restrictions upon use of IMF Funds*

Although there are several restrictive regulations regarding the use of IMF funds, the Agreement has provisions for relinquishing all or part of such restrictions (Article V, Section 4). For example, special consideration is given to members with a record showing avoidance of large or continuous use of IMF's resources, also to members in need of periodic or exceptional requirements, and, if necessary in such cases, it is stipulated that the IMF may demand of the members concerned gold, silver, securities or other assets as collateral security.

In their initial operations, the IMF authorities assumed a comparatively rigid attitude toward the use of their resources by members, but later, owing to the little use made of the Fund, they relaxed their attitude and gradually came to apply the waiver clause to many members' use of IMF funds.

Thus, since 13 February 1952, the Executive Directors have observed the following basic principle :

1. Each member may count on receiving the full benefit of any doubt respecting drawings which would raise the Fund's holdings of its currency to not more than its quota. (As the quotas of members had been paid to the extent of 75 per cent in their respective currencies and the balance in gold, the above ruling is tantamount to an unconditional permission for members to use IMF funds to the extent of their gold subscriptions. It may be remembered that this part of the IMF's holdings is called the gold *tranche*.)
2. The IMF would take a liberal attitude towards the use of funds up to the point at which it would hold not less than 100 per cent (25 per cent plus 75 per cent) or not more than 125 per cent of that member's quota (this 25 per cent margin is called the first *tranche*), provided that the member concerned were making every effort to find a solution of its balance of payments problem.

As a result, it is now almost a general rule for the use of funds up to 50 per cent (gold *tranche* and first *tranche*) of a member's quota to be approved comparatively easily.

In keeping with the foregoing relaxation of restrictions, the Executive Directors introduced on 1 October 1952 a new technique for the use of funds, the so-called stand-by-credit, of which an explanation will be given in a later chapter.

(e) *Restriction upon Member Qualifications*

Lastly, we shall touch upon a member's qualification for using IMF funds. A member is qualified to make use of IMF funds when it has fixed the par value of its currency (Article XX, Section 4 (*b*)).[1] It would however be restricted in, or become ineligible for the use of IMF funds, in the following cases :

1. If it changes the par value of its currency, in spite of the objection of the Fund in those cases in which the Fund is entitled to object (Article IV, Section 6).
2. If it uses the resources of the IMF in a manner contrary to the Fund's purposes (Article V, Section 5).
3. If, after being requested by the Fund to exercise appropriate controls for the prevention of the use of the Fund's resources for capital transfers, it fails to do so (Article VI, Section 1 (*a*)).

4. Adjustment of Imbalances of Members' Accounts

The IMF is designed to assist in the adjustment of temporary disequilibrium in a member country, so that it is clearly desirable that there should not be prolonged resort to its facilities. Moreover, as the IMF was set up as a joint exchange fund with the subscriptions of members, its resources extend only to these subscriptions which are based upon their quotas. The funds in the possession of the IMF were therefore from the very beginning in the nature of a revolving fund; unless those supplied return to the IMF, there is a danger that it might cease to function. This is why the IMF has taken the following measures in order to adjust the imbalances in members' accounts :

(a) *Imposition of Charges*

The first measure to be mentioned is the imposition of charges. Generally speaking, a member buying the currency of another from the IMF in exchange for its own currency has

---

[1] The regulation that a member only becomes eligible to make use of IMF funds when it has established the par value of its currency has been relaxed for some countries. For instance, Indonesia, with a currency of no fixed par value, receives funds from the IMF on the basis of a provisional exchange rate on condition that it will make appropriate adjustments when the par value of its currency has been fixed. Peru, also, though it is a country with no fixed par value for its currency, having adopted the floating-rate system, has been granted stand-by-credits.

each time to pay to the IMF $\frac{1}{2}$ per cent (the initial charge of $\frac{3}{4}$ per cent was reduced to $\frac{1}{2}$ per cent in November 1951) as a service charge. In addition, it has to pay a charge calculated according to the average daily balances of its currency held by the IMF in excess of its quota. The greater the amount and the longer the period of these holdings the larger will be the rate charged to prevent them from increasing. Alterations were made in November 1951, and again in December 1954, in order to be able to charge less for a short and higher for a long term.

If a charge accumulates and reaches a rate of 4 per cent per annum, the member concerned must consult the IMF about the measures to be taken to reduce the drawing. Though the charge (and the service charge) should in principle be paid in gold the currency of the member may be used in part payment if its currency reserves are less than one-half of its quota.

In this connection, it may be recalled that when a stand-by-credit, is arranged a fee of $\frac{1}{4}$ per cent is levied. This will be included in the service charge when drawings on the credit are made.

(b) *Repurchase by Member of its Own Currency*

We now come to an adjustment measure which is more important than the imposition of charges. A member may repurchase its own currency, as provided by Article V, Section 7 of the Agreement, which specifies the conditions under which it may be required to repay its borrowings. This section provides that, where the Fund's holdings of its currency exceeds its quota, a member may repurchase part or all of it for gold. Moreover, a member is obliged to repurchase its own currency from the IMF for gold or for a convertible currency (which is also called an Article VIII currency) at the end of each IMF financial year, subject to certain conditions. These are that, in principle, a member is required to repurchase one-half of the increase that has occurred during the year in the IMF's holdings of its currency and, that it is also required to add to the above repurchase one-half of any increase that has accrued during the year in its monetary reserves. If, however, there is a decrease in its monetary reserves, it is then permitted to deduct one-half of the decrease from the above repurchase. Therefore, should the decrease in the member's monetary reserves during the year exceed one-half of the IMF's holdings of its currency, there will be no necessity of repurchase at all. None of the adjustments mentioned above shall be carried to a point at which

1. the member's monetary reserves fall below its quota;
2. the IMF's holdings of its currency fall below 75 per cent of its quota, or
3. the IMF's holdings of the currency required to be used for the repurchase exceed 75 per cent of the quota of the member concerned.

So much for the basic principles concerning the repurchase by a member of its own currency. It may not be amiss in this connection to add that the IMF Executive Directors, adopted on 13 February 1952 the following resolution regarding repurchase:

1. In those cases in which it would appear appropriate and useful the IMF might arrange drawings to deal with special short-run situations accompanied by arrangements for repurchase in a period not exceeding eighteen months.
2. Exchange purchased from the IMF should not remain outstanding beyond the period reasonably related to the payments problem for which it was purchased from the IMF. The period should fall within an outside range of three to five years.

As we know, the repurchase by a member of its own currency should be made with gold or a convertible currency. This does not mean, however, that gold or any convertible currency will do for the purpose. Schedule B attached to Article XX of the Agreement has fixed the proportions of currencies to be used for repurchase as follows:

1. If the member's monetary reserves have not increased during the year, the amount payable to the IMF shall be distributed among all types of reserves in proportion to the members' holdings thereof at the end of the year.
2. If the member's monetary reserves have increased during the year, a part of the amount payable to the IMF equal

to one-half of the increase shall be distributed among those types of reserves which have increased in proportion to the amount by which each of them has increased. The remainder of the sum payable to the IMF shall be distributed among all types of reserves in proportion to the member's remaining holdings thereof.

The measures for the strict specification relating to the types of monetary reserves to be used for repurchase are not wholly clear. We may note, however, that the application of this regulation puts the Fund into a somewhat complicated position in international monetary affairs. For instance on 3 November 1960 France repurchased $130 million of its own currency and, as at that time the proportion of gold in its monetary reserves had increased remarkably, it had in accordance with the above regulation to pay in gold for the greater part of this repurchase and, to raise the necessary funds, it was obliged to buy gold from the United States authorities in exchange for dollars; this further decreased America's gold reserves which had already fallen, owing to the prevailing mistrust of the dollar. Then, to offset this new decrease the IMF sold $300 million of its own gold holdings and bought American treasury bills with the proceeds.

(c) *Declaration of Scarce Currency*

If despite these measures the IMF's holdings of a particular currency become exiguous the final and drastic measure is to declare it to be 'a scarce currency' (Article VII). Thus, if the demand for the currency of a member is such that the Fund is convinced that its ability to supply it is threatened, it shall formally declare that currency to be scarce. Once such a declaration has been made, the IMF shall apportion it to members with due regard to their relative needs, the general international economic situation, and any other pertinent considerations. At the same time, following consultations with the IMF, members will be temporarily authorized to impose discriminatory restrictions upon exchange dealings in the scarce currency.

Prior to this declaration, however, the IMF has authority to replenish its holdings of a scarce currency by taking the following two measures. First the IMF may buy scarce currency from the member concerned with the gold in its possession. This means that there is no possibility whatsoever of a declaration of scarce currency being made for currencies other than those of leading countries. The reason is this: the smaller the country, the smaller will be its subscription to the IMF, and so the capacity of the IMF to supply currency would be less in the case of a small country. In practice however, demand for IMF funds tends to be for the currencies of leading countries, which are international currencies, and, even if a demand for those of small countries arises temporarily, the IMF can easily cope by buying them in exchange for the gold in its own possession. Therefore, the currencies that can possibly be declared scarce are limited to those of certain leading countries. When the IMF was established the currency expected to become scarce was the U.S. dollar because the discrepancy between other countries and the United States, whose economy had expanded greatly as a result of the Second World War, was expected to lead to an active demand for U.S. dollars, and that demand was in turn expected to exceed the capacity of the IMF to supply even with the mobilization of all its holdings of U.S. dollars and gold. As a measure against such a world-wide shortage of dollars, the following clause was inserted in the IMF Agreement.

This, the second measure to be taken before the declaration of a scarce currency, has come to assume a role of great importance. It is the regulation that the IMF may borrow the scarce currency from the member concerned or, with that member's approval, from some other source. Here, the member concerned is under no obligation to make such loans to the IMF or to approve the borrowing of its currency by the IMF from any other source, but it seems reasonable to suppose that, when the IMF Agreement was signed, the other countries persuaded the United States, the world's greatest creditor country, to choose between a positive lending policy toward the rest of the world, or discriminatory exchange restrictions at the hands of all other countries. This clause, however, has never been invoked even during the post-war period of dollar shortage, for direct aid under the Marshall Plan and other arrangements has been freely given by the United States to all members. Further, the firm attitude taken by the IMF to protect its resources when agreeing to the request of members for dollar funds has so reduced the demands on the Fund's holdings of gold and dollars as not to necessitate a declaration of scarce currency. On the other hand members, other than the United States, have been permitted to resort to exchange control under the provisions for the post-war transitional period, and have thus been able to cope with the dollar shortage by taking appropriate measures against the United States, without the necessity of such a declaration.

Section 5.—Organization and Management

The structure of the IMF is described in Article XII of the Agreement, and consists of a Board of Governors, Executive Directors, a Managing Director and a staff.

1. Board of Governors

The Board of Governors is the highest decision-making organ of the IMF, and consists of one governor and one alternate appointed by each member, in such manner as it may deem appropriate. Each governor and each alternate should serve for five years subject to the pleasure of the member appointing him, and may be reappointed. The Board of Governors shall select one of the Governors as Chairman.

The Board of Governors may delegate to the Executive Directors authority to exercise any powers of the Board, except the power to:

1. Admit new members and determine the conditions of their admission.
2. Approve a revision of quotas.
3. Approve a uniform change in the par value of the currencies of all members.
4. Make arrangements to co-operate with other international organizations.
5. Determine the distribution of the net income of the IMF.
6. Require a member to withdraw.
7. Decide to liquidate the IMF.
8. Decide appeals from interpretations of the Agreement given by the Executive Directors.

The Board of Governors shall hold an annual meeting and such other meetings as may be deemed necessary by the Board or called by the Executive Directors. Meetings of the Board shall be called by the Directors whenever requested by five members or by members having one-quarter of the total voting power. The Executive Directors, at their discretion, may obtain by mail a vote of the Governors on a specific question without calling a meeting of the Board. Governors and alternates shall serve as such without compensation from the IMF, but the IMF shall pay them reasonable expenses incurred in attending meetings.

A quorum for any meeting of the Board of Governors shall be a majority of the Governors exercising not less than two-thirds of the total voting power, and, except as provided otherwise, shall make a decision by a majority of votes. The Board of Governors shall have a chairman and two vice-chairmen, who shall be selected by vote at the preceding annual meeting of the Board and serve as such for one year.

2. Executive Directors *report to Board of Governors*

The Executive Directors shall be responsible for the conduct of the general operations of the IMF, and for this purpose exercise all the powers delegated to them by the Board of Governors. They need not necessarily be governors.

There shall be not less than twelve directors, which total may be increased with the approval of the Board of Governors when governments of other countries become members. Five of the directors shall be appointed by the five members having the largest quotas (being called appointed directors), and the others shall be elected by the members other than the above-mentioned (being called elected directors). Of the elected directors, two shall be elected from the American Republics not entitled to appoint directors, and the rest from the other member countries. In addition to the above directors, two members, the holding of whose currencies by the IMF have been, on the average over the preceding two years, reduced below their quotas by the largest absolute amounts, shall be granted the right to appoint a director. (An example is Canada.) The election of elective directors shall be conducted at intervals of two years, and if the office of an elected director remains vacant more than ninety days before the end of his term, another director shall be elected for the rest of his term by the members who elected the former director.

The Executive Directors shall function in continuous session at the principal office of the IMF which, according to Article XIII of the Agreement, shall be located in the territory of the member having the largest quota (it is now in Washington), and should meet as often as the business of the IMF may require. The Executive Directors shall select a Managing Director, who shall be chairman of the Executive Directors. Except in special cases, the chairman shall call a meeting of the Executive Directors at least with two days' clear notice. A quorum for any meeting of the Executive Directors shall be a majority of the directors representing not less than one-half of the voting power. Each appointed director shall be entitled to cast the number of votes allotted to the member appointing him and each elected director shall be entitled to cast the number of votes which counted towards his election. Each director shall appoint an alternate who will exercise the director's voting power when the director himself is not present. A member not entitled to appoint a director may send a representative to attend any meeting of the Executive Directors when a request made by, or a matter particularly affecting, that member is under consideration.

3. Managing Director

The Managing Director shall be selected by the Executive Directors and become their chairman, but should have no vote except a deciding vote in case of an equal division. He shall be chief of the operating staff of the IMF and shall conduct, under the direction of the Executive Directors, the ordinary business of the IMF and, subject to the general control of the Executive Directors, shall be responsible for the organization, appointment and dismissal of the staff of the IMF.

The Managing Director is normally to be appointed for five years, but this may be altered by the Executive Directors. Any qualified person who is younger than 65, shall be selected as Managing Director and when he reaches the age of 70, he shall resign his office. Incidentally, past Managing Directors of the IMF have been Camille Gutt (Belgian) for the years 1946–51, Ivar Rooth (Swede) for the years 1951–56, and Per Jacobsson (Swede) for the years 1956–64.[1]

4. Voting Power

Each member shall have two hundred and fifty votes, to which shall be added one additional vote for each part of its quota equivalent to one hundred thousand United States dollars.

5. Other Matters of Operation

The structure of the IMF is as described above, and we give below some information concerning its business management. The business year of the IMF originally began on 1 July and ended on 30 June, but these dates were changed to the 1 May to 30 April as from the financial year 1958–59.

The expenditure required for the running of the IMF is financed from the charges for services levied when use is made of the IMF resources, and a financial statement expressed in U.S. dollars and accompanied by a statement of its auditors shall be presented to the Board of Governors each year.

The Executive Directors, on 25 January 1956, decided that it should be possible to invest the Fund's gold amounting to $200 million in U.S. Treasury bills of 93 days' tenor or under and did so, after having taken measures for the repurchase of their gold and the maintenance of the gold value. This investment was for the purpose of raising financial resources required for defraying the various operating expenses of the Fund. On 24 July 1959 this investment was extended to U.S. Treasury bills of less than one year and raised to $500 million. Further, on 8 December 1960, gold valued at $300 million was also sold to the United States for similar investments. But the other aspect of such an operation was temporarily to supplement the U.S. gold reserves.

[1] Mr. Jacobsson died on 5 May 1963. *Repo's*

VII

POLICY OF THE INTERNATIONAL MONETARY FUND

MORE than sixteen years have elapsed since the IMF commenced operating in March 1947. This has been a period during which most of its members have had to apply exceptional regulations to deal with the post-war transition. It may be said, therefore, that the IMF has had to face situations that those who drafted the Agreement did not at all expect and that it has displayed flexibility in doing so. Although some reference has already been made to these questions in Chapter VI, we shall now discuss them more fully.

1. Exchange Rate Policies

The first question the IMF had to handle was the establishment of initial par values. The procedure to be followed is laid down in Article XX, and in consequence on 18 December 1946 the Fund requested its members to communicate their par values of exchange based upon their exchange rates prevailing on 28 October 1945, that is, sixty days before the entry into force of the Agreement. Thirty-two members (that is, all thirty-nine members less those which applied for postponement) made the required communication to the IMF. The par values communicated, however, were those which had been in force before the Second World War, so that it was clear, in view of the rising tendency of commodity prices experienced in many countries during the war, that most of the par values, though different in degree, were overestimated as against the U.S. dollar. The Fund raised no objection, however, and recognized them as the initial par values. In view of the stress that the IMF Agreement placed upon the stabilization of exchange rates, why did the Fund tolerate the failure of members, when choosing their initial par values, to adjust for over — or under — valuation of member's currencies ; and why did it allow them to take the easy-going attitude of keeping them at the uniform level prevailing on 28 October 1945? The reasons are as follows:

First, in many countries there was at that time no scope for exchange rates to perform the function of promoting exports and restraining imports. Those countries which had suffered great damage on account of the Second World War were in varying degrees unable to reconstruct their economies, or even to maintain their normal economic position without dependence upon the enormous productive power of the United States. Under those circumstances, their exports were influenced not so much by their price as by productive capacity; alterations in exchange rates were therefore unlikely to lead to significant increases. Nor were variations in exchange rates likely to bring about a contraction in imports, as these consisted mostly of foodstuffs, raw materials, reconstruction goods and the like, commodities so urgently needed that they could not be reduced. It could in fact be said that the maintenance of over-valued exchange rates was in certain respects desirable in order to maintain domestic activity and to promote economic reconstruction.

Second, if exchange depreciation had been enforced, it would have aggravated the inflation in the countries concerned and would also have accelerated their shortage of dollars at that time by worsening their terms of trade.

And, third, despite the above-mentioned circumstances, it was necessary by establishing par values to place the exchange rates of members under the control of the IMF.

For the above reasons, the IMF made no objection to the exchange rates communicated so long as they did not exercise unreasonable pressure upon the exports of the members concerned. Their initial establishment, therefore, was not based upon the expectation that they would be maintained for very long, but that they would naturally be adjusted if, after the restoration of members' productive power, their exchange rates could again promote exports and restrain imports. Thus, the adjustment of these initial par values was carried out when the par value of the pound was reduced by 30·5 per cent (that is, from $4.03 to $2.80 to the £1) on 18 September 1949, and the par values of the greater part of the countries of the non-dollar area were also adjusted whole-sale.

Countries that reduced their par values numbered 25, of which 18 were members, *viz.* Australia, Austria, Belgium, Britain, Canada, Denmark, Egypt, Finland, France, Greece, Iceland, India, Iraq, Italy, Luxembourg, Norway, the Nether-lands and the Republic of South Africa, and 7 non-mem-bers, *viz.* Argentina, Burma, Ireland, New Zealand, Portugal, Sweden and West Germany. The adjustment affected coun-tries that handled 65 per cent of the value of total world trade.

The provision in the IMF Agreement for the regulation and use during the post-war transition and the adoption from the outset of a system of placing exchange rates under its control by the obligation upon members to establish par values, demonstrate that the Agreement had profited from the inter-war period, when international exchanges were in disorder. The Agreement consequently placed the greatest emphasis upon the stabilization and orderly adjustment of exchange rates, which had in fact been the intention since the White Plan. Throughout the sixteen-year period, from the time when exchange rates were placed under the control of the IMF to the present day, there has never arisen a situation under which competition in the reduction of exchange rates has flourished. Thus, generally speaking, the intention of the IMF of bringing about stabilization and an orderly adjustment of exchange rates may be said to have been fully achieved, but, at the same time, experience has revealed the following defects in the IMF's parity system :

1. With the recovery in members' productive powers, there were indications that their par values had from about the beginning of 1948 begun to exercise pressure upon their exports, and the IMF, in its annual reports, clearly showed that it welcomed the reduction of their par values ; but the only members that changed their par values prior to the devaluation of the pound in September 1949 were Colombia and Mexico. The reasons for the hesitancy of some members appear to have been the question of procedure, and the difficulty of deciding the level of their respective new par values, since in the present Agreement no provision is made

for the IMF to propose a change of par value in any positive manner.

2. This being so, the par values of some members have been maintained for a long time.

Once the decision is made to alter the par value, the member concerned naturally seeks to reduce it drastically to avoid being compelled to carry out another reduction in the near future. This is borne out by the fact that the devaluation of the pound in 1949 was as high as 30·5 per cent in spite of the expectation that it would only be devalued by 20 to 25 per cent.

3. In principle a change of par value is recognized as valid only when there is a fundamental disequilibrium, but in the case of such a broad adjustment as in 1949, there would be no time for investigation, since delay in reaching a decision would inevitably lead to speculation in the currencies concerned, with all its attendant confusion.

4. Furthermore, making obligatory the establishment of initial par values uniformly for all members was bound to make the par values of some members meaningless in due course.

When the initial par values were established, fifteen countries had adopted multiple exchange rates, and the IMF recognized as their initial par values rates selected from the range of those in use. These par values, however, became widely separated from the relevant market rates as a result of various measures subsequently taken by these countries. For example, in the Argentine, Chile and Paraquay, no exchange transaction is at present effected at a rate based upon the par value, and in Brazil the exchange rate applied to imports in general is ten times higher than its par value. In short, the establishment of par values in these countries is purely nominal.

This does not mean, however, that in the past the IMF has kept unconditionally to the principle of par value so favoured in the Agreement. On the contrary, its policy has been very elastic; it has taken into consideration the situation of member countries, and has not paid excessive attention to the consistency of its policy with the provisions of the Agreement. First, it has sometimes postponed for a considerable time the fixing of a par value for countries that had applied for it.

At the end of May 1960 there were still thirteen countries the par values of whose currencies had not been fixed; they were Afghanistan, Cyprus, Indonesia, Korea, Laos, Liberia, Malaya, Nepal, Nigeria, the Republic of China, Thailand, Tunisia and Vietnam. Second, and more important, a flexible or floating rate system has been permitted. Whenever special circumstances have existed, the IMF has so far been ready to relax the principle of fixed exchange rates provided for in the Agreement, and has recognized either system at the request of its members.

Canada, for example, faced in September 1950 with an inflow of American capital due to the Korean War, experienced increasingly inflationary tendencies. It therefore abandoned its initial par value of 1.10 Canadian dollars per U.S. dollar and adopted a floating rate system, which the IMF is said to have willingly approved. Mexico also proposed that, before the establishment of its new par value, it should for a time let its currency fluctuate on its exchange market so that an appropriate level for its par value might be evolved, and this also had the Fund's approval. The IMF also recommended the multiple exchange rate system countries to shift from their multiple exchange rates to a floating rate as a step toward the simplification of their system, and promised aid in case of necessity. Thus, the regulations for the conduct of exchange transactions with the Fund for members with floating rates were officially laid down on 15 June 1954. It cannot be said, however, that this meant that the IMF had abandoned its principle regarding fixed rates; it merely meant that it recognized floating rates as a provisional measure to deal with special circumstances. When the IMF approved the adoption of floating rates, the member gave a definite undertaking to establish a fixed rate as soon as possible, and also accepted the obligation to hold close consultations with the Fund during the continuance of floating rates.

2. Exchange Restrictions and the IMF

As already stressed, the freedom of current exchange transactions constituted the basis of the IMF system, and its main functions, such as its drawing facilities and the adjustment of exchange rates, were all designed for that purpose.

Each member, therefore, being obliged under Article VIII of the Agreement to maintain the convertibility of its own currency held by another member, is at the same time required in principle, not to impose restrictions upon payments for current transactions nor to resort to any discriminatory currency measures. The fact is, however, that immediately following the Second World War, members all suffered from a serious shortage of dollars and foreign currencies and, therefore, if exchange transactions had been left entirely free, the stabilization of exchange rates and the equilibrium of international payments would have been doomed to failure. The IMF Agreement therefore provided in Article XIV for a post-war transitional period, and freely permitted its members to impose exchange controls temporarily in order to deal with the special situation arising from the dollar shortage. This transitional period was at the outset to last for five years following the institution of the IMF, that is up to February 1952; in practice, until 1960, there were only ten members, all on the American continent, that had accepted the obligations of Article VIII.

In the Agreement, there are two cases where the adoption of exchange control may, in general, be permitted. In addition to the transition period there is the case of a scarce currency. This has already been discussed. The reasons for the inability of members to abolish their exchange controls differed in detail, but common to all was the shortage of dollars. It follows that if the IMF had been permitted to declare the U.S. dollar a scarce currency and to enforce exchange restrictions solely against it, then the imposition of exchange restrictions in general based upon Article XIV would have been abandoned by many member countries much earlier than proved to be the case. In fact, however, the Fund took preventive measures to restrict its supply of U.S. dollars before its holdings became scarce; in consequence, despite the serious dollar shortage, its holdings of U.S. dollars were not reduced sufficiently to justify the declaration of a scarce currency. The period of exchange control restrictions allowed by Article XIV therefore continued for a long time after the war. In this situation, however, the countries of Europe wished to allow as much liberalization of their exchange transactions as possible and, as a result, the OEEC countries formed the European Payments Union (EPU), which contributed a great deal to the realization of this end. Seen from this angle, therefore, the establishment of the EPU was in practice tantamount to the declaration by the European countries that the dollar was a scarce currency. Indeed, it may be said that what had not been achieved by the IMF was realized by the European countries on their own initiative.

Second, the important question confronting the IMF in the midst of this continuance of exchange restrictions was that of the confusion of cross rates. When currencies of various countries have an external convertibility, some order in the various cross rates is naturally established by arbitrage. The IMF system, however, did not begin with external convertibility as an indispensable condition. Each member under Article XIV could therefore take advantage of the postponement of external convertibility, but was nevertheless under the obligation, in accordance with Article IV, Section 3, of maintaining its foreign exchange rates with other currencies within the limit of 1 per cent above and below the par value of its own currency. This contradiction is well brought out in the opposing views of France and the IMF. France's trade structure for several years before the war was characterized by an excess of exports over imports with Britain and an excess of imports over exports with the United States. In consequence, if it had been able to cover its excess of imports from the United States with sterling acquired from Britain, it would have been in a very favourable position. As, however, the pound at that time was not convertible, this was not possible. France, therefore, was compelled to accumulate a large amount of inconvertible sterling, and at the same time was faced with a growing imbalance in its dollar position. To cope with this situation, France was obliged to allow a wide variation between the rates for the dollar and for sterling.

On 25 January 1948 France devalued from F.119 to F.214 per dollar and at the same time set up a free exchange market in addition to the official market. It also took measures obliging exporters to the dollar area to sell half the proceeds of exports at the official rate, and the other half at the free market rate. Importers from the dollar area had to buy one half of the currency required at the official rate and the other half in the free market, except for certain commodities. For sterling transactions, however, the official rate applied to both exports and imports, so there was no possibility of avoiding confusion in the cross rates. (For example, at the end of October 1948 the effective rate of the franc stood at about F.262 per U.S. dollar and at F.864 to the pound. In consequence, the cross rate came out at $3.28 to the pound, which was very much below the official rate at the time of $4.03.) These French measures, considered unavoidable as a means for preventing an accumulation of inconvertible sterling, were contrary to the IMF Agreement, which requires the maintenance of exchange rates within 1 per cent of the par value of their currencies. As a result, France was deprived of the right of using the resources of the IMF for five years up to 15 October 1955. Thus, up to 29 December 1958 — when its new par value was fixed — France was in the position of having no par value approved by the IMF.

Though the operations of the IMF during the transitional period were not considered altogether satisfactory, the efforts it made during that period to obtain world-wide liberalization of exchange rates should not be treated lightly. Toward the end of 1958, the West European countries succeeded in obtaining external convertibility, and in February 1961 they began to prepare for compliance with Article VIII, all of which was possible only because of the improvement in their respective economies. Nevertheless it cannot be denied that the IMF contributed greatly to the realization of the general improvement. Some of the IMF's contributions were as follows:

1. Even allowing that the stabilization of exchange rates was formally achieved, it would be meaningless if exchange transactions themselves were still under direct control. Here the IMF authorities, though adhering to the principle of fixed rates, proposed to some countries that they should adopt a floating rate and, by supplying stabilization funds where necessary, induced many countries to change from direct to indirect control. Countries which took that course were Argentina, Ecuador, Paraguay, Peru and Uruguay.

2. When in the fourth quarter of 1956 as a result of the Suez Crisis the pound was in a critical condition, the IMF took the unprecedented step of making a loan to Britain amounting to 100 per cent of its quota in one amount, thus preventing sterling, an international currency, from reverting to an intensification of exchange restrictions.

3. Since 1952 the IMF authorities have held annual consultations with Article XIV countries concerning the removal of exchange restrictions, and have continuously given them advice on the same matters.

3. Lending Policies

The supply by the IMF of foreign currencies, should, in principle, be an automatic procedure so long as it is conducted under the terms of the Agreement. In the beginning, however, when most of the members were suffering from a dollar shortage, the enforcement of those provisions concerned with drawings of foreign currencies might have paralyzed this function of the IMF. Consequently before the Fund commenced operations, the Managing Director announced that for the time being drawing of foreign currencies would be allowed only on condition that (1) they would be limited to member countries in which a currency crisis existed and that the use of IMF resources gave some prospect of settling that crisis; and (2) the purchase of foreign currencies by members would be subject to investigation by Fund officials. Thus, from the beginning, the IMF's function of supplying foreign currencies was deprived of its automatic character and came under its complete control and discretion. Despite those restrictive measures and the prevailing balance of payments difficulties, full use was made of IMF resources, so much so that during the year 1947 alone, the year in which IMF activities began, the amount drawn reached as much as $467 million. Once, however, the Marshall Plan had come into operation, in 1948, restrictions on the use of IMF resources became more severe. The Executive Directors, with the intention of preserving IMF funds, limited their use to the minimum thought necessary to leave them with enough resources to cope with the demand that was expected to arise after the plan came to an end; thus on 5 April 1948, they served notice on all members to the effect that those which had participated in the Marshall Plan should only purchase U.S. dollars from the IMF in exceptional or unforeseen circumstances. Aid under the Marshall Plan was given on the basis of the actual requirements of each European country, and, if they were already receiving aid from the IMF, assistance received under the Marshall Plan was reduced by that amount. In this sense, it may be said that the Fund's restrictive policy at that time was a very useful measure. As a result, the use of its resources by members greatly declined, so much so that in 1950 there were no drawings at all. With the Marshall Plan coming to an end in June 1951, however, this IMF policy was relaxed and various measures were taken to this end. At first, the use of IMF resources, which had been directed towards the relief of currency crises, was directed towards achieving the objectives of the Agreement. Thus, a resolution of the Executive Directors passed on 2 May 1951 made it clear that the IMF would ungrudgingly grant funds to facilitate members' plans for the realization of economic stabilization designed to secure monetary stability, the adoption of realistic exchange rates, the relaxation and removal of restrictions and discrimination, and the simplification of multiple currency practices. Further, the IMF announced in February 1952 that even although a member did not immediately make use of the drawing authorized, it could do so whenever it needed the funds in the course of carrying out its plans. This became a permanent formula when, in October of the same year, the Executive Directors published their general principles concerning stand-by-credits. This stand-by-credit, as has already been explained, is an arrangement under which, when authority has been given for a particular amount, the member does not draw the full amount, but only the sums required from time to time during the period fixed up to the limit granted. The stand-by-credit made it possible for a member to have IMF funds as secondary reserves. Though there are still restrictions as to both period and conditions, the automatic character of the use of IMF funds, lost at the beginning of the Fund's operations, was now partially restored. In this sense, it was indeed a noteworthy measure. In addition to this there was the relaxation of quantitative restrictions upon drawing facilities. As already mentioned, the Executive Directors of the IMF, by their resolution of February 1952, had made it clear that full approval would be given to a request for funds with respect to that part of the IMF's holdings of the currency of a member which did not exceed its quota, that is, the gold *tranche*, and also with respect to 25 per cent of the excess of the IMF's holdings of the currency of a member over its quota, that is, the first *tranche*. Further, should a request be found reasonable, funds beyond these limits would be supplied. Acting along these lines and commencing with Turkey in August 1953, the IMF often invoked this waiver clause, and supplied each year funds surpassing 25 per cent of the quota of the borrowing member. Moreover, although the supply of funds is based in principle upon the prior establishment of a par value, Indonesia, which had not fixed its initial par value, was nevertheless supplied with funds in 1954 under its provisional official exchange rate; and in June 1954 arrangements were made for transactions between the Fund and members with floating rates. (This is also discussed in Chapter VI, Section 4).

Quite apart from these relaxations, the Korean War, which had broken out in June 1950, resulted in a great mitigation of the dollar shortage, so that the supply of IMF facilities remained at a rather low level until 1955. It is true that the reaction to the Korean boom in 1952–1955 was the main cause of drawings to a total of $315 million, but, generally speaking, in every year since 1950 there was an excess of repayments over new borrowings, as a result of which outstanding borrowings, which had amounted to $757 million at the end of 1949, fell to $234 million at the end of 1955. At this time, however, members' balance of payments difficulties had not yet been overcome, and in consequence the enforcement of exchange control persisted as tenaciously as before. That the demand for IMF funds nevertheless remained small could be partly attributed to apprehension that application for assistance would draw attention both at home and abroad to their difficulties, with the consequence that the receipt of aid from the IMF would aggravate rather than improve their position. At the same time there was rising criticism of the Fund, which is reflected in its annual reports during the period. One proposition was that members should make more use of IMF facilities to achieve the objectives of the Agreement. In 1956, however, the situation underwent a complete change. The volume of funds made available during the year 1956 (May 1956–April 1957) reached the unprecedented total of $2,075 million, of which $862 million were drawings and $1,212 million stand-by-credits. Further, the loans granted were all in convertible currencies (with the exception of the purchase by Egypt of Canadian dollars, equivalent to $15 million, they were all in U.S. dollars), and as the gold and dollar assets of the IMF at the beginning of that fiscal year stood at about $4,300 million, the available gold and dollar assets of the IMF, if the stand-by-credits not yet utilized be taken into account, decreased by one-half in that year.

The Suez Crisis was responsible for the reactivation of the IMF. Britain and other members faced a serious crisis over their reserves, and the Fund resorted to a bold lending policy to remedy the situation. As bearish speculation was rampant at the outbreak of the Suez incident, the IMF decided to supply funds at once to Britain up to an amount of 100 per cent of its quota, that is, $1,300 million (of which, $738 million was by a stand-by-credit), a move that alleviated the sterling crisis, and incidentally silenced the critics.

When the thirteenth annual meeting of the Board of Governors was held at Delhi in October 1958, it was against this background that the representative of the United States proposed an increase of quotas by 50 per cent, and this was formally approved on 2 February 1959. The current quotas are on that basis.

Since February 1961, when some leading West European members adhered to Article VIII, the lending activities of the Fund have undergone an important change in policy. As these matters are related to the question of the reform of the Fund, they will be examined in Chapter IX, Section 2.

VIII

SALIENT FEATURES OF THE INTERNATIONAL MONETARY FUND AND ITS PROBLEMS

THOUGH founded on international co-operation, the IMF, which reflects the intricate relations between members, cannot help incorporating some half-measures and contradictions. When its structure is surveyed we shall find that its affinity to the gold standard and its consequent limitation stand out as its most serious drawbacks.

Apart from its effectiveness in practice, the IMF, as is clear from the discussion of its origin in Chapter V, was from the beginning intended to achieve the systematization of a gold standard-like constitution. Though Keynes said that it was the opposite of a gold standard system, this was very much a political view (Chapter V, Section 5). The IMF was in fact originally designed to influence the world economy in the monetary sphere, and therefore could scarcely avoid having some of the characteristics of the gold standard.

Conflicting interests and opinions gradually distorted and weakened this original inspiration. In consequence, it is not surprising that the IMF developed into a somewhat shadowy and inadequate international monetary organization. We shall now look more closely into the circumstances and influences which allowed the IMF to drift into its current situation.

The first thing to note is that the IMF has attached the currencies of its members to gold and required the establishment of gold parities.

This, we know, came from the apprehension felt during the 1930s regarding the instability of currencies unattached to gold, and from the stipulation in the Agreement that the par value of a currency shall be expressed 'in terms of gold as a common denominator or in terms of the United States dollar of the weight and fineness in effect on 1 July 1944', thus causing the dollar parity to take the place of a gold parity.

This is the inevitable result of the fact that the IMF is not the controller of gold; that is, it is not a real focus for international payments, and cannot in itself be an international monetary system. The truth is that it has merely a supplementary function based upon the dollar standard system, because the currencies of members are linked with the dollar and not with gold. It may therefore be said that the gold parity in the IMF is a fiction without any supporting facts. Moreover, for an international gold exchange standard system to work smoothly through the IMF, it is necessary that the dollar should have the characteristics of a gold standard currency. But in fact, what do we find? We find that the convertibility of the dollar into gold is limited, and its gold value is not of an absolute character. Herein lies one of the contradictions of the IMF and also one of the elements leading to the instability of currencies, for the clauses of the IMF concerning the establishment of par values are based upon the supposition that the U.S. dollar is intrinsically a gold standard currency.

Next, by limiting the fluctuation of foreign exchange rates to within 1 per cent above and below parity, the IMF adopted a so-called par value system or a fixed rate system (Article IV, Section 3). This regulation was not explicit nor very concrete, but, as mentioned in Chapter VI, Section 2, it was made clear on the institution of the European Monetary Agreement that these limits were required only in respect of the dollar rate. On the other hand, the IMF stipulates in its Agreement and Regulations that when a member deals in gold, its price should be within 1 per cent above par when it buys and within 1 per cent below par when it sells. Here 'a member' means the monetary authorities of a member, and buying or selling means buying or selling for monetary purposes.

The regulations seemingly set no limit on sales by a member above or buying below par value, but should the other party be the monetary authorities of another member, they are prohibited from buying gold above and selling below par value, which means that the transactions between the two are restricted to within a certain margin above and below par value.

This is a natural measure so long as the Agreement treats gold and the U.S. dollar as equivalents. The IMF Agreement, we know, provides in Article V, Section 6, that (a) any member desiring to obtain, directly or indirectly, the currency of another member for gold shall, provided that it can do so with equal advantage, acquire it by the sale of gold to the Fund, but (b) nothing in this section shall be deemed to preclude any member from selling in any market gold newly produced from mines located within its territories. Clearly this provision is based upon the existence of a free gold market: the Agreement has no provision whatever in respect to non-monetary gold. This is yet another contradiction.

It will be recalled that during the inflationary period immediately following the war, the purchase and sale of gold between countries with a premium and the granting of subsidies to gold-producing mines were common practices, thus giving proof of a double gold price system on a global scale. However, the IMF requested its members in June 1947 to cease purchasing and selling gold with a premium and in the following December published its views concerning subsidies. These were based on the argument that, if transactions in gold are effected directly or indirectly, at prices that will cause a weakening of exchange rates, the stability of international payments will be jeopardized. Subsidies were prohibited only (a) when granted uniformly and (b) when they jeopardized the stability of foreign exchange. It would appear that in all other cases they were officially recognized as valid, whatever their form. In this way, the IMF speedily took its first retrograde step in its gold policy.

The prohibition of the purchase and sale of gold with a premium was not effective, however, and so the IMF was compelled to take a further retrograde step. Thus,

1. In June 1948 France legalized a free internal gold market in Paris, but this market maintained semi-official connections with overseas countries through such operations as smuggling. The IMF had no choice but to acquiesce in this.
2. The IMF annulled their system of interfering in gold for processing or semi-processing.

Thus, in September 1951 the IMF, bowing to the inevitable, issued an epoch-making statement concerning its gold policy. It ran:

'Despite the improvement in the payments position of many members, sound gold and exchange policy of members continues to require that, to the maximum extent practicable, gold should be held in official reserves rather than go into private hoards. . . . However, the Fund's continuous study of the situation in gold-producing and consuming countries showed that their positions varied so widely as to make it impracticable to expect all members to take uniform measures to prohibit a premium on gold. Accordingly, while the Fund reaffirms its belief in the economic principles involved and urges members to support them, the Fund nevertheless leaves the practical decisions involved in their implementation to its members.'

Though it was a circuitous statement, it meant that the IMF officially recognized as valid the purchase and sale of gold under premium. And in its annual report of the following year, the IMF virtually abandoned its gold policy, conceding that:

'The only effective way of getting rid of premium gold markets and private hoarding of gold over a period of time is to create the economic conditions under which the demand for hoarding will become negligible.'

Such being the case, international transactions in gold lapsed almost into chaos (except for dealings at the official price in the United States). Ironically enough, it was the reopening of the London gold market in March 1954 that saved the situation and introduced some degree of control. The reason was that London was traditionally an international market where the greater part of the free gold transactions of the world was concentrated, and prices there were controlled indirectly by the official prices in the United States and the shipping parity. That is, so long as the U.S. Government agreed to buy or sell gold at $35 an ounce plus or minus a certain amount of commission, the prices quoted on the London market are automatically restricted to the official price plus or minus the expense of shipment between London and New York. (Should the purchase or sale be accompanied by a mere accounting transfer, then even the above expense could be disregarded.)

Under current conditions, this regulation is far from perfect, because, when the U.S. Government buys gold, it does so from any party without limit, but it sells gold only to the monetary authorities of foreign countries. As a result, though the lower limits of the London quotations are rigidly regulated, their upper limits are not so strictly controlled. If, therefore, demand from outside the monetary authorities is stepped up for some reason or other, the upper limits will be practically non-existent.

The abnormal rise of prices in the London gold market in October 1960 was a result of such conditions. The IMF adopted a neutral attitude, stating that, as non-monetary gold transactions, they were not their concern. This attitude was logical, for it had already ceased to interfere in view of its lack of power to do so. The London market, however, did not necessarily distinguish between monetary and non-monetary transactions; moreover, as a great international market, it could not remain indifferent to transactions made outside the official price. This explains why the British and American authorities decided to co-operate : it was reported that they reached an agreement whereby the Bank of England itself should endeavour to stabilize prices, the drain on its gold reserves being replenished by the United States. In this way the United States attempted to meet its responsibility as the final controller of gold. The outflow of gold from America accelerated, however, with the result that stocks accumulated for monetary purposes, fell into the hands of hoarders.

The above events illustrated the drawbacks in the control over gold which were inherent in contemporary international monetary arrangements.

Again, the IMF Agreement allows for occasional changes in fixed exchange rates, and for a relaxation of the rigidity of the gold standard. The basic principle of changes in par values in the IMF seeks to make such changes orderly so that, under a floating rate system, an exchange stabilization fund will fix rates at appropriate, equitable, levels.

The application of this formula in the Agreement is, however, somewhat asymmetrical in the following cases :

1. The establishment of an exchange par value in the IMF is in many cases carried out under cover of various exchange restrictions and it is therefore questionable whether it reflects the true strength of the currency concerned.[1] Moreover, in contrast with the floating-rate system under which the authorities concerned are allowed sufficient scope to ascertain the equitable level, by taking into consideration the trend of the market, there is no such provision under the fixed rate system; in consequence, there is the risk that those exchange levels may differ from the true position.

2. The position of the IMF regarding a change of par value is entirely passive, and so there is no possibility of an appropriate change being based upon equitable judgment.

The next question arising from the gold standard-like character of the IMF is that of the convertibility of currencies as between members, and their convertibility into gold.

According to the IMF Agreement, the convertibility of the currencies of members into gold is a one-way traffic, and it is only indirectly achieved by acquiring through the market such currencies as are in fact capable of being converted into gold. Moreover, the convertibility of the currencies as between members is limited by the restrictive exchange control regulations. These characteristics weaken the contention that the IMF is of a gold standard type.

Professor Nisaburo Kito suggests that the one-way convertibility of gold does not invalidate the equivalence between gold and currency. Even under the gold exchange standard system, the amount of currency created is limited by the gold and dollars held, and currency is normally never changed into gold. But even if currency is not changed into gold, this does not mean that currency is created arbitrarily. As the exchange rate of a gold standard country under the gold exchange standard is fixed and exchange is sold without limit, the equality of value between currency and gold is, in some sense, much more perfect than under the original gold standard system.

[1] It is doubtful to what extent this situation was rectified by the adjustment of the par values of members in 1949. Moreover, it must be borne in mind that at that time members were clinging to their trade and exchange restrictions.

So we may ask : what is the true extent to which the IMF may supply foreign exchange? Under this system, certainly, limits are set upon the purchase of foreign currencies, but mis-understanding could arise through exaggeration of the differ-ence between this and the free sale of exchange under the gold exchange standard system, because, although under the gold exchange standard gold exchange was sold without limit, the volume of the sales was automatically restricted by a strict regulation of the volume of currency. Likewise, limits to the purchase of foreign currencies under the IMF system are set by the manner of control by members, and so there is no inherent difference between the two. In other words, the utilization of IMF resources does not mean that it is possible for a member to buy foreign commodities in exchange for its own currency, nor that the offer of a piece of paper is given a purchasing power in foreign countries.

A member's borrowing from the IMF should have a counterpart in the export of its own merchandise, though some time lag may be involved. To the extent that a member can temporarily sustain an excess of imports over exports, while maintaining its exchange rate and suffering no worsening of its terms of trade, the use of IMF resources is undoubtedly a facility for the member concerned, but is is a mistake to regard it as more than that.[1]

That gold is not used in IMF transactions certainly does not lessen its resemblance to a gold standard. The situation is similar to that of the gold exchange standard system. Nor can it be denied that the gold standard characteristics of the IMF are closely connected with its other functions, as elabo-rated below.

The view that member's currencies are equivalent to gold pervades the Fund Agreement. In this sense, all currencies are equal. On this point, Harrod says : [2] 'The first systematic attempt to establish a world-wide gold standard, in which a large number of the adhering nations are, in theory at least, equi-pollent, has been that of the International Monetary Fund. Its troubled career to date has been attributed to the

[1] Nisaburo Kito, *Sekai Tsuka no Shorai*, pp. 42-6. Published by the Akagi Shobo.
[2] R. F. Harrod, *Gendai-no-Pondo*. (The Japanese version, published by the Shiseido, p. 4.)

148

vast dislocations of the post-war period, and that is in the main correct; but it is also possible that its difficulties have been aggravated by the fact that we just do not know, for lack of experience, how a gold standard can or ought to work when adhering members are supposed to operate as if they were equi-pollent.'

However, it is stipulated in the Agreement as mentioned in Chapter VI, that the gold value of its assets should be maintained by all means, and that its gold assets should be expanded at all possible opportunities.

For a gold standard-like system to work smoothly, however, as we have learned over the years, a firmly-established gold centre is essential. If there had been no centre, as in London, it is very doubtful whether the gold standard system would have been able to measure up to the description given of it in any textbook to which reference may be made.[1]

The IMF is not, however, a perfect currency system in itself. Though it was originally intended to have the character of a gold standard, yet, owing to its system of one-way traffic in gold and to the lack of automatism in the supply of funds and of its power to control credit, it lacks the prerequisites of a gold centre. The controller of gold is not the IMF, but New York. In this sense, the U.S. dollar and the currencies of other members cannot be of equal status. This is the reason for the wide discrepancy between the above-mentioned theory and reality. The position has not yet been reached in which all members are of equal strength.

In consequence, whether the present world currency system, including the IMF, is able to function smoothly or not, depends entirely upon the United States' capacity of controlling gold. Should this capacity be weakened, the insecurity and instability of the whole organization becomes manifest.

When gold recovered its dominance, a noteworthy event took place. On 25 January 1956 the Executive Directors adopted a resolution to the effect that in the event of there being a deficit in its financial accounts, the IMF should be empowered to buy U.S. Treasury bills with its gold and effected many operations as mentioned on page 129.

The recent sale was clearly made with the intention of

supporting the U.S. dollar, and may be regarded as quite exceptional. If, however, the IMF were to undertake such quasi-open market operations more often, it would be violating the basic principle of one-way traffic in gold. The real meaning of such an action, however, was that the IMF was reinforcing the dwindling capacity of the United States to control gold and was assuming its role as a gold centre.

Next, the gold standard of the IMF type is also contradictory on the following point. We know that the IMF has adopted the fixed rate system. The maintenance of this requires members' commodity price levels to be harmonized. The achievement of this harmony in turn requires a symmetry such as is found in the gold standard system. The IMF structure, however, does not ensure this; it has been likened by a certain writer to 'a recipe to go swimming without getting wet'.[1]

If there is a key to these contradictions, it is to be found in the manner in which the IMF provides funds; but its character is not suited to an active creation of international credit — if anything, it is rather negative.

To explain this further: when a member pays 25 per cent of its quota in gold and the balance in its own currency, it merely means that in respect to this 25 per cent the ownership of the gold has been transferred from the member concerned to the IMF. If no drawing on these assets is in fact made, there can only be a decline in international liquidity by so much gold being rendered inactive.

Next, the payment of the 75 per cent in the member's own currency may have been taken to mean, at least at the beginning, that so much was added to international liquidity (in the sense that drawing on the funds was made internationally); but it could only be drawn once, and what followed had to depend upon an increase in its quota, for 'the acquisition of foreign currencies by a member from the IMF in exchange for its own currency is nothing but the exchange of an equivalent and should not be regarded as the granting of credit'.[2]

That is, if the currencies of members are all considered the

---

[1] G. N. Halm, *International Monetary Co-operation*, p. 125.
[2] Nisaburo Kito, the above-mentioned book, p. 37. (Explanation of the White Plan.)

equivalent of gold, the 75 per cent of their quotas means an increase in the volume of gold, and then the subsequent transactions are only an exchange of gold for gold.

If, therefore, an increase in the quotas is made in keeping with a change in the volume of world trade, then there will be no decline in liquidity, but if not, the possibility is that the system will easily bring about a decline as mentioned above.

Thus, if the adjustment of disequilibrium is placed upon the shoulders of debtor countries, the danger is that it will lead to a low-level equilibrium.

This is another way of saying that under the IMF system elasticity is not inherent inside the Fund but should exist outside. It was partly due to such a situation that, following the war, the United States was compelled to finance international credit by enormous external assistance, for the United States, fearing that the provision of credit within the IMF organization would expand to too great an extent, wished to provide credit at its own discretion outside that organization.

IX

FUTURE OF THE
INTERNATIONAL MONETARY SYSTEM

Section 1.—Toward a Reform of International Monetary System

THE weakening of America's balance of payments, the instability of sterling, and the revaluation of the Deutsche mark — this latest series of events in international monetary affairs has underlined the drawbacks of the present organization. It is, therefore, not surprising that voices have been raised in favour of a re-examination of the international monetary system.

The arguments for reform have hitherto been directed towards international liquidity, that is to the question of the capacity of current international arrangements to supply sufficient external settlement funds to support the expanding trade of the world. Criticism of the present form of the IMF in this respect began with the outbreak of the Suez incident, and has been going on ever since. The crises brought about by this event (in July 1956) in the foreign exchanges were corrected by the enormous sums advanced by the IMF, but this, while demonstrating its utility, has created no small apprehension as to its future activities. Thus, throughout 1957 as a result of the large funds supplied by the IMF for relieving Britain and other members of their serious foreign currency difficulties, its uncommitted holdings of gold and dollar funds sank to the low level of $1.2 billion, if the unused part of the stand-by-credit be taken into consideration; in this way the role of the IMF as a second-line foreign currency reserve for members was to that extent diminished. It is not surprising that this situation led to discussion about international liquidity, and the IMF itself, responding to the request of some of its members, instructed its staff to make a thorough examination of the matter. The results of the IMF investigation were published in August 1958, under the title of *International Reserves and Liquidity*. Though the views disclosed may not necessarily be official, yet they may be taken as reflecting the thought of the Fund's authorities. The following is the gist of the report:

'Fundamentally, a country's payment for the importation of commodities and services from abroad is ultimately made from the receipts from its exports and services to countries overseas. At any one moment, however, many countries are liable to suffer from disequilibrium in their balance of trade. These difficulties may sometimes result from a change in world trade conditions, and sometimes from intrinsic factors at home. Whatever the cause, measures of some kind should be taken to rectify the imbalance. Some delay will unavoidably occur before these measures take effect, and during this time recourse is usually made by the country concerned to its external reserves. At this stage we have to ask ourselves whether the foreign currency reserves of almost all the countries in the world would be sufficient to act as a cushion against a virtually universal unfavourable balance of payments.

'It would be correct to say that whether or not these gold and foreign currency reserves would be sufficient is, of course, a question for the individual appreciation of each country concerned, but the relationship between total reserves and the total volume of world trade should also be considered. At the end of 1957, the ratio of the world's official gold and foreign currency reserves (excluding those of the Communist bloc) to world imports was 51 per cent. In the past the ratios have been 21 per cent in 1913, 42 per cent in 1928 and 100 per cent during the years 1937–1938. Therefore, the current rate of liquidity is higher than in 1928 and lower than in 1937–1938. The adequacy or not of international liquidity cannot in fact be deduced from a comparison between reserves and world trade, for the existence of a low ratio will not prevent the smooth conduct of world trade, provided that balance of payments difficulties are not acute; while, if the ratio is high, it would constitute a serious impediment to international trade if such difficulties were great. Again, at such times, the reserves of the countries concerned would not need to be

particularly large if corrective measures were speedily introduced, while failure to do so would necessitate the possession
of fairly large reserves. Furthermore, in the case of unfavourable balances of payments, the existence or non-existence of an
international credit organization, would acquire added importance in deciding upon a suitable level of external reserves.

'From this we may infer that in assessing the optimum
degree of international liquidity various economic influences
and conditions must be taken into consideration, not merely
the ratio between reserves and the volume of world trade.
This may be seen from the fact that of the three periods
mentioned above, international trade was conducted most
smoothly and orderly in 1913 when the settlement reserves of
the world were smallest. In other words, the world economy
as a whole functioned smoothly under the gold standard
system, even though international reserves were small.

'In 1928, however, though the ratio of external reserves to
the volume of trade was higher, the world economy stood on
the brink of a catastrophe. Further, in 1937–1938, despite the
unprecedentedly high level of reserves, there was no stimulus
to the expansion of world trade. The fundamental reason
was that, after the First World War, the world economy
disintegrated, as did the gold standard system, which had up
to that time made possible orderly international settlements.
With the end of the gold standard, all countries cut their
currencies adrift from gold and introduced whatever monetary
policies they desired. Some went so far as to resort to unhealthy inflationary measures in their domestic finance while
their exchange rates, which had lost the stabilizing support of
a gold standard, underwent violent fluctuations, resulting in a
good deal of competitive exchange depreciation. Under these
circumstances, tariffs and other trade restrictions became
general. Thus the restriction of imports by one country led
to retaliatory measures by another, and world trade steadily
shrank. Moreover, since the First World War, New York had
added to its stature as an international financial centre, and
international finance tended gradually to be divided between
the two centres of London and New York, which, however, has
not necessarily brought about good results. The division into
two of the international financial market has resulted in funds,

that had hitherto centred smoothly on London, being moved to and fro between the two cities for monetary or political reasons, and thus possibly disturbing normal international finance. The conclusion to be drawn from experience acquired since the First World War is that the influence of reserves upon the expansion of world trade is not as great as was expected and that the general trend of trade was not to be decided by the mere factor of liquidity. To try to measure the adequacy of international liquidity by comparing reserves and trade in recent years with those in the past is to treat the subject too superficially. In support of this assertion, we may note that the greater volume of reserves in 1937–1938 compared with those of the present day, were required to deal with a much larger number of unfavourable factors. Indeed, if we exclude the years before 1914, when the gold standard system worked smoothly, the current degree of liquidity has become more favourable than that in 1928. Moreover, if the degree of balance of payments difficulties and the collapse of an international credit organization are taken into consideration, the surmounting of such difficulties has become far easier now than then. This is despite the fact that the ratio of reserves to the volume of trade has never been lower than during the past few years.

'Further, the polarization of gold in the United States of America, which became more intense during the inter-war years, has since 1949 been reversed, with the result that the increased reserves of countries outside the United States have helped to make a far more healthy situation in international liquidity.

'However, even if, as some say, the present degree of liquidity is sufficient, world reserves should be reinforced to keep pace with future increases in trade. There is no historical evidence, however, for supposing that there is a precise mathematical correlation between the expansion of trade and the increase in reserves. It is true that a slight increase in total reserves against an expansion of trade may be justified, but the future should be able to take care of itself, in so far as the output of new gold is incorporated in monetary reserves to the extent of some $700 million, and to the extent that foreign currency holdings are expected to increase. There is also a vast amount of private short-term credit which offers good hopes for the future reinforcement of liquidity. This short-term credit mechanism, though less powerful than before the First World War, when confidence in currencies was much stronger, is now better equipped than during the inter-war period and that immediately following the Second World War. Moreover, its scope is expected to widen further as mutual confidence in currencies increases, and controls are relaxed. Such an increase of private credit is also expected to lighten considerably the burden borne by the world's official reserves. In addition to all this an international credit organization, the IMF, has now been firmly established. It may therefore be supposed with reason that the future of the world's reserves will not be as dark as some people predict.

'To say this, however, does not mean that there is no dark side at all to the question of reserves. The fact we have to face at this juncture is that those members which have in the last few years reinforced their reserve positions are mostly the advanced industrial countries, while the reserves of the less advanced nations have, speaking generally, tended to worsen owing to such factors as large-scale development programmes, a decline in raw material prices, and chronic inflation.

'To cite a few examples, during the period from 1948 to 1957, the ratio of reserves to imports declined from 84 to 48 per cent in Ceylon, from 195 to 43 per cent in India, from 37 to 1 per cent in Bolivia, and from 120 to 69 per cent in Uruguay. It is, of course, essential that such countries should take domestic measures to rectify these unfavourable tendencies, but it is also necessary for the IMF to consider their requests for assistance. The Fund's present gold and dollar resources for such purposes amount to only $1.4 billion, so that it is questionable whether they will be adequate to discharge its responsibility in the future. This pitiful condition of the Fund is attributable primarily to the basing of quotas on the pre-war economy. Thus, though the volume of world exports fell by 7 per cent from 1937 to 1947, in the next ten years it increased by 90 per cent, a rate of expansion almost unknown in the past, and the prices of internationally traded goods increased by 140 per cent between 1937 and 1957. World trade has, therefore, advanced remarkably from the conditions prevailing at the time of the Bretton Woods Conference. It could be said that if all countries made every effort, by well considered policies, to achieve economic equilibrium, to avoid increasing obstacles to trade, and to strengthen the international credit organization, then the question of reserves in the coming ten years would not be particularly difficult to solve.'

It is clear from the above that the basic idea of the IMF authorities at that time seems to have been that, to deal with the question of international liquidity, it would be sufficient to raise the quotas of members whenever necessary and to reinforce the development of international finance and the capital market, through convertibility on the foreign exchange markets. Thus, the policy of the IMF authorities for settling the question of international liquidity consisted simply of expanding IMF funds and did not envisage any fundamental reform of the present organization. To carry out this idea a proposal to increase the quota of members was approved at the annual meeting of its Board of Governors held at New Delhi in 1958.

While the IMF held to its way of thinking, there were some who insisted upon the need for a fundamental reform of the organization. As will be discussed later, Sir Oliver (now Lord) Franks, then Chairman of Lloyds Bank, proposed a so-called Franks Plan in his annual statement for 1958, and Maxwell Stamp, formerly an adviser to the Bank of England, put forward a so-called Stamp Plan in *Lloyds Bank Review* in October 1958. When towards the end of 1958 the West European countries decided to restore current convertibility, Professor Robert Triffin of Yale University, fearing that disorder in the international monetary system would result from this restoration, published the well-known Triffin Plan in the March and June numbers of the Quarterly Preview of the Banca Nazionale del Lavoro.

This Triffin Plan was designed to bring about a thoroughgoing reform of the present international monetary system. Though the plan will be examined in a later section, his basic idea is outlined below :

Following the expansion of world trade, it has now become impossible to depend upon gold only for international reserves. The ratio of gold reserves to the total value of world imports has already declined from 110 per cent in 1938 to 40 per cent in 1958, and the supplies of gold for monetary uses to be expected for the whole free world in the future will only amount to about $730 million a year, even if the new output of Soviet Union gold and its sale by that country are taken into consideration. This yearly increase represents only 1·5 per cent of the reserves of the entire free world of today, while world trade is at present expanding at the rate of 5-6 per cent a year. With gold alone, therefore, the world will never be able to maintain a sufficient level of reserves against the expected expansion of trade. The current international monetary system is the so-called gold exchange system under which the United States of America allows conversion into gold of the U.S. dollar balances held by foreign authorities, and Britain and other West European countries permit conversion into U.S. dollars of non-resident holdings of their own currencies while the remaining countries hold these convertible currencies in addition to gold in reserves. Under this system, therefore, the shortage of gold is being supplemented by the convertible currencies of leading countries, such as the dollar or the pound. This gold exchange standard system, however, contains a grave functional drawback. Under this system, anxiety has only to be felt about the future of, say, the dollar, for immediate and incessant drawings on the dollar deposits of all countries to result, and international liquidity would suffer a rapid decline. Even should no such apprehension be experienced and should the dollar deposits of all countries tend to grow, the external short-term liabilities of the United States would increase, and weaken to that extent its gold reserve position.

If, therefore, the dollar deposits of all countries were considerably to surpass the gold reserves of the United States, this would in itself lead to anxiety about the dollar. This being the case, even if an increase in dollar deposits may be said to make up for the shortage of gold in the world, there must naturally be limits to such developments. If dollar deposits increase over this limit, suspicion of the dollar would hasten conversion into gold of these dollar deposits, thereby causing a decline in international liquidity.

This means that the present gold exchange standard system is not a suitable method of supplementing the shortage of gold. As long as this system is maintained, the possibility cannot be excluded that the world economy would sooner or later, owing to the shortage of reserves, repeat the experience of the 1930s *i.e.* devaluation, strengthening of exchange control and general deflation.

The above is the essence of Triffin's reason for the reform of the present international monetary system. His fears regarding the gold exchange standard system were soon given a practical demonstration in the instability of the dollar in 1960, and of the pound sterling in 1961, with the result that serious discussions began concerning the reinforcement or reform of the present IMF organization.

Examination of the various measures proposed for the reinforcement or reform of the IMF seems to show that there are two basic approaches to the question of international liquidity. One of these stresses the problem of imbalance, and the other that of the total volume of liquidity. Those who are optimistic about the future liquidity situation believe that it will suffice to correct imbalances as soon as possible and they do not, therefore, insist upon any fundamental reform of the present system; while those who are pessimistic take up the question of how to preserve adequate liquidity and, in consequence, hold that, as this is inevitably connected with the questions of a centre of international finance and of a credit control system, there should be a reform of the present dollar standard system.

These arguments for reform, therefore, may be divided into the following three groups:

1. The current question can be solved within the framework of the IMF Agreement, and, even if an attempt be made to reform it, it should be done slowly and progressively. Such a view is called, provisionally, an argument for Conservative reform.
2. Another view adovcates a progressive and important reform of the present Agreement. This is named an argument for Positive reform.
3. It is necessary to make a fundamental re-examination of

the present Agreement and reform the IMF itself. This may be labelled an argument for Fundamental reform.

We shall in the following sections study the arguments as classified above.

In addition to these proposals, there was another for a return to the gold standard system advocated by Jacques Rueff, economic adviser to President de Gaulle, and Professor Michael Heilperin. In brief, they point to the elements of instability inherent in the present gold exchange standard system, which has national currencies such as the dollar and the pound as international currencies, and insist upon its abolition and upon a return to the complete gold standard system of former days. However, they put forward no concrete proposals for dealing with the liquidity shortage to be expected from a return to the gold standard system. Here, we merely mention the existence of this viewpoint, without, however, going into details.[1]

Moreover, there is another measure which is capable of solving the problem without resorting to a reinforcement or reform of the IMF system as suggested above. It is an increase in the price of gold consistently advocated by Sir Roy Harrod. This proposal is no doubt very attractive to those who are pessimistic about the future of international liquidity. We shall give its details in Section 4 when discussing the question of reform of the IMF.

Section 2.—Suggestions for Conservative Reform

As can be seen from 'International Reserves and Liquidity', a report made by the staff of the IMF, the IMF authorities themselves are in the vanguard of conservative reform. The late Per Jacobsson, then Managing Director of the IMF, appeared to hold the opinion that a reform of the present organization was unnecessary. He asserted that the achieve-

[1] Rueff's views on this question are expressed in his article 'Un Danger pour l'Occident: The Gold Exchange Standard' in the issues of *Le Monde* for 27-29 June 1961, and also in his article 'The West is risking a Credit Collapse' in the July 1961 number of *Fortune*. The views of Heilperin are given in 'Für eine atlantische Währungsordnung' in the 10 September issue of *Neue Zürcher Zeitung*.

ments of the IMF had hitherto been quite remarkable, and
that some of the matters now claiming attention can be solved
within the present system. The fact is that the IMF has
hitherto not been able to give the fullest expression to its
original functions, owing to the persistence of exchange control
in member countries, but it may now be said to be in a position
to do so, owing to the restoration of convertibility, the liberalization of trade, and the transfer of many members to Article
VIII status. In view of these developments, therefore, if the
policies of the IMF are flexible enough, they should be able
to meet any future requirements. This was Jacobsson's view
and that of other responsible officials of the IMF.

That there is a strong demand for reform of the present
monetary system, can, however, be seen from the special
message by President Kennedy (at the beginning of 1961) on
the international balance of payments. The IMF authorities
felt compelled to make a substantial proposal of some kind,
and the matter was discussed at a meeting of the Executive
Directors held in February 1961. The resolution adopted,
called the Jacobsson Plan, is, not surprisingly, of such a character as not to alter the Agreement itself directly, but merely
to make the utilization of IMF funds more flexible. As the
reinforcement of IMF funds under the current structure was
subject to intricate formalities where an increase in the quotas
of members was concerned, and as, further, their distribution
was dependent on individual negotiations despite the existence
of a system of stand-by-credits, this plan sought to lessen
existing rigidities; it would allow a more speedy mobilization
of funds from creditor countries and their prompter distribution
amongst debtor countries in need of them.

This is based upon the Bernstein Plan, the proposal put
forward by Edward M. Bernstein, former Director of the
Research Department of the IMF. We shall now examine
this.[1]

The Bernstein Plan consists of two basic parts. The first
concerns the measures to be taken for relieving the balance of

[1] The so-called Bernstein proposal is described in 'International Effects of
U.S. Economic Policy', Study Paper, No. 16, 25 January 1960, pp. 84-6, presented
by Edward M. Bernstein to the Joint Committee of Congress of the United States,
and his paper 'The Adequacy of United States Gold Reserves' presented to the
American Economic Association on 30 December 1960.

payments difficulties of key countries, which are brought about by the international movement of short-term funds. In essence the IMF would issue debentures to creditor countries, thus borrowing their surplus funds, and lend these funds to debtor countries under a simple procedure. As an example, should gold flow out of the United States and concentrate in West Germany, the IMF would issue debentures and borrow Deutsche marks, which they would then lend to the United States. The U.S.A. would then purchase those dollar balances held by the IMF with these Deutsche marks. The debentures issued by the IMF would be payable on a fixed date, interest-bearing and exchange-guaranteed. The issue of those debentures would only be made if the IMF considered that it was actually confronted with an urgent demand for funds. The debenture holders would be allowed to request redemption before their maturity dates. This, it is hoped, would offset the present tendency for each country to accumulate dollar balances and to convert them into gold, causing in consequence a large outflow of gold from the United States.

Bernstein then proposes that there should be set up a separate account named 'Reserve Settlement Account', through which the above-mentioned operations would be carried out, so that they do not cut across transactions properly appertaining to the IMF, and so that they do not run counter to the Fund's basic principle that advances should not be made for balance of payments difficulties that result from an outflow of capital. Moreover, this account should be permitted to conduct business such as depositing, earmarking, lending and borrowing, and the buying and selling of gold.

We would agree that if the IMF debentures were convertible into gold this would constitute a worthwhile reform of the present system. It brings to mind the Bank for International Settlements of former days and the functions of a Stabilization Fund, as proposed by the White Plan (Chapter V, section 2). Furthermore, Bernstein's proposal, as he himself claims, will be able to maintain organic relations between the financial centres and does indeed deserve the description of 'a logical completion of the Bretton Woods System'. That the proposal is of a negative character is due to the fact that it does not create credit at all, which goes to prove that the IMF is not capable of being the controller of credit, or, otherwise expressed, is not capable of being the controller of gold.

In short, the proposal can be regarded as a further attempt to introduce into the IMF organization the flexibility of mutual exchange of currencies, but, as this flexibility does not have the character of a clearing union, it cannot be denied that the proposal has considerable limitations. Consequently therefore, Professor Robert Triffin criticizes the proposal as follows : [1]

First, the proposal is simply a half-way reform plan designed to correct short-term disequilibrium. It is therefore not only useless as a long-term solution of the question of international liquidity, but tends also to evade its essential point.

Second, the IMF in mobilizing funds from members, has to follow complicated procedures such as entering into individual negotiations and obtaining the approval of a member's Parliament upon the uncertain basis of its future balance of payments with the result that the IMF would not in practice enjoy much mobility. It is wiser to simplify the present Agreement as a whole and thereby avoid the trouble of individual amendments and periodical negotiations.

Third, if the IMF were to issue its debentures for general purposes, it would be in the irrational situation of possessing a large amount of local currencies which are not actually used for international payments.

In response to this latter criticism, Bernstein dropped the proposal to issue debentures for public subscription, and proposed the following : measures to relieve balance of payments difficulties which are occasioned by capital movements should be the concern only of the leading advanced countries, and the projected Reserve Settlement Account should conclude with them an agreement permitting the Account to receive stand-by-credits within certain limits; the above account should, when necessary, borrow currencies from creditor countries against interest-bearing notes, and immediately lend the proceeds to the leading debtor countries. In this case, the Reserve Settlement Account becomes merely an in-and-out

[1] Robert Triffin, 'The International Monetary Crisis: Diagnosis, Palliatives and Solutions', *Quarterly Review and Investment Survey*, First Quarter, 1961. 'Altman on Triffin, A Rebuttal,' Hearings before the Joint Economic Committee, Congress of the U.S. 86th Congress, Second Session, 7, 8 December 1960, by U.S. Government Printing Office.

account, and is therefore never in possession of any funds; but in order to safeguard the funds to be borrowed and lent against the risk of a subsequent change in the value of currencies, they should be secured by a gold guarantee. Bernstein suggested that the limits of borrowings from leading countries should be as follows: $3 billion from the United States, $1.5 billion from Britain; and $3.5 billion collectively from Belgium, Canada, France, Italy, Japan, the Netherlands and West Germany, the total amounting to $8 billion.[1]

The second part of the Bernstein Plan concerns the promotion of positive policies for lending which is the original function of the IMF. The following features should be noted:

1. The lending policy hitherto operated by the IMF has involved the unconditional approval of loans up to 25 per cent of a members' quota (gold *tranche*), it has granted loans comparatively freely for the next 25 per cent (first *tranche*), but has been strict in extending advances beyond this. By changing its policy the Fund should make it possible for members to draw automatically without its approval, so long as they remain within 25 per cent of their quota each year.

2. This would enable members to make free use of their respective quotas so that they may consider their transactions with the IMF not as special advances, but as ordinary daily transactions; in consequence, instead of using their own reserves, they could draw on IMF funds for external payments to an equivalent amount and, when they increase their foreign currency reserves, they may pay the equivalent to the IMF for the repurchase of their own currencies.

3. At the same time, members may incorporate into their foreign currency reserves the equivalent of those maximum drawings which are permitted under the current IMF regulations.

4. Under Article V, Section 3, (*a*) (i), of the Agreement, it is stipulated that 'the currency is presently needed for making

[1] The idea that the IMF should obtain stand-by-credits from advanced countries is said to have been suggested by Xenophon Zolatas, Executive Director of the IMF and President of the Bank of Greece, and is also named the Zolatas Plan.

payments in that currency', but the IMF should take steps to neutralize this condition by applying section 4 of the same article. That is, although under the above stipulation a member in need of dollar funds can only draw on those of the IMF, this has lost its significance with the restoration of convertibility and the adherence of many members to Article VIII ; it is wholly reasonable that in order to promote one of the prime objectives of the IMF — multilateral transactions in the currencies of members — it should make advances in currencies such as, for example, Deutsche marks which are not needed, at least, for the present, and exchange them as convenient for currencies required on foreign exchange markets.

Such is the gist of the Bernstein Plan, and part of it has already been implemented by the IMF authorities in their subsequent operations, *i.e.* the policy of increasing the number of currencies in which loans may be granted as described in (4) above. Since 1960 the policy of the IMF has been to lighten the burden of the United States by spreading its loans over the currencies of those countries which adopted convertibility and which are comparatively rich in reserves, instead of making them only in U.S. dollars, which was its former practice. The first instance of this change was when the IMF, granting an advance to Yugoslavia of $75 million in December of the same year, spread the amount to be lent over British pounds, Deutsche marks, French francs, Italian lire, Netherlands guilders and U.S. dollars. The same thing happened when advances were granted to Australia, Brazil, Britain and India in 1961. It may even be said that, with the adherence of many West European countries to Article VIII, the policy of granting advances in multiple currencies has now become a normal business operation of the IMF.

The IMF authorities have also adopted with some amendments to those measures for the relief of balance of payments difficulties experienced by key countries due to short-term capital movements, which are basic to the Bernstein proposal. In view of the fact that under the IMF Agreement it is stipulated that advances should not be made when balance of payments difficulties were caused by capital movements,

Bernstein, as already stated, had proposed the institution of a 'Reserve Settlement Account' to deal with this situation. Later, however, the Executive Directors of the IMF, applying a looser interpretation of its regulations concerning capital transactions provided by Article VI of the Agreement, adopted a resolution to the effect that, should any member confronted with an outflow of capital ask for its aid, the Fund would be ready to agree, provided that the member country had taken suitable measures to prevent the outflow, and that the borrowing be repaid within a period of from three to five years. In this way, measures to relieve international monetary difficulties arising from the movement of short-term funds have been effected within the ordinary framework of the IMF (Vienna meeting), without the creation of a separate 'Reserves Settlement Account'. Against such a background, agreement was reached, at the sixteenth annual meeting of the IMF in September 1961 (Vienna meeting), upon arrangements to enable the Fund to borrow from ten leading countries up to $6 billion in their currencies for the purpose of increasing its resources in case of necessity. Although this proposal met some strong opposition from France, the Netherlands and Belgium, it was nevertheless finally approved, in principle, and the Executive Directors were requested to formulate a definite plan by the end of 1961. As this demonstrates, the current tendency is to achieve the desired objective by a looser interpretation of the provisions of the Agreement, and to alter the organization as little as possible. This is no doubt a very realistic way of dealing with the matter, but it is also very negative.

Section 3.—Suggestions for Progressive Reform

In contrast with the proponents of a conservative reform of the present organization, there are many who advocate a decisive and progressive re-casting of the present Agreement to meet the present situation. The best and most logical argument for reform is in an article titled 'International Reserves and Liquidity' by Thomas Balogh, of Oxford University, in the June 1960 number of *The Economic Journal* (pp. 357-88).

Balogh first severely criticizes the IMF staff's report outlined in the preceding section. He asserts that the report is
based upon the quantity theory of money and is not backed by
any clear rational reasoning. The report's prime object, he
says, is to preserve international reserves and thereby to
exercise immediate direct influences upon economic activities.
This is far from being the fact, however; according to Keynesian analysis the most important thing is expenditure, not its
monetary image. He goes on to say that the report holds that
international capital movements are necessarily of a balancing
character and overlooks the essential fact that the volume of
reserves needed is also determined by the character of an
external disequilibrium. Moreover, although the report is
pervaded by the idea that in a period of depression only
debtor countries should take control measures and that IMF
funds should be used only to give them a breathing space,
one would expect some recognition of the fact that it serves
only to impart a deflationary bias to the world economy. It
is also strange that nothing is said about the scarce currency
clauses. Finally, it is taken for granted that, although the
absolute volumes of international trade and industrial production have increased, their rates of expansion since 1948 have
declined continuously. Further, the report fails to make any
observations on the effect its analysis would have in hindering
economic growth and the achievement of international
equilibrium.

In short, it seems that the report neither acknowledges, nor
is indeed aware, that if the rate of increase in international
liquidity falls below the desirable rate of expansion in production and trade, it is necessary to have agreements designed to
add continuously to liquidity. Thus the report, after a long
series of statistical exercises, which aim to show that the increase
in monetary reserves need not be as high as the expected rate
of economic growth, concludes that it is rather doubtful
whether the present funds at the disposal of the IMF, in
relation to the rate of expansion of trade, are sufficient to
enable it to discharge its responsibilities efficiently, and
recommends that the quotas of members be raised, as they
were subsequently.

What, then, is the basis for the contention that international reserves are inadequate? It depends upon the objectives of economic policies and upon the role to be played by external reserves in conjunction with other measures in their realization.

1. In the first place assessment of the reserves required is dependent upon the content of policies, and especially by the limits set to them by unemployment and a slowing in the rate of growth.
2. At present, world trade is concentrated in a few major countries, and therefore the report is correct in its assumption that, if a sound policy is carried out, a small reserve will be adequate. This, apparently, is based upon the further assumption that, if the major countries reduce their levels of employment, other countries will follow suit.

   Under a system which allows the movement of capital, as at present, though it be of a speculative character, larger reserves are required than under a system that forbids it. What determines the volume of reserves required is the extent of instability, as well as the amount, of external payments. Furthermore, the world economy is a kind of oligopoly, so that, whenever any change occurs, each country tries to adjust its policy in relation to the others. For example, if gold flows out of the United States, all other countries seek to acquire it, thereby encouraging a shortage of reserves.
3. The acquisition of international reserves is a kind of sacrifice in the sense that it stops investment (or consumption). This sacrifice can be justified by using reserves only to pay for imports if it enables that country to increase the growth of its economic activity and investment over a period of time, despite disequilibrium in its balance of payments.
4. The accumulation of foreign currency reserves instead of gold increases international liquidity and so, relatively speaking, has an inflationary impact. If, therefore, this arises under conditions of full employment, and countries with financial centres disregard the increase of their liabilities, the result is apt to be general inflation. If, however, the exchange of foreign currencies for gold develops in a significant degree then the pressure is likely to be deflationary.

5. Where there is a general lack of liquidity, no country would find it possible to permit the loss of gold, and so there would arise an oligopolistic struggle; the attempt of each country to increase its reserves would cause a general deterioration and would not only contribute nothing to the improvement of the reserves position of any individual country, but would also produce deflationary pressure on the whole front. The only relief in such a situation would be either to raise the price of gold or additional internationally acceptable means of payment.

6. So long as a country which has lost reserves continues to operate policies that cause a deficit in its international balance of payments, no addition it can make to its reserves will ever be sufficient. Additions to reserves under an inflationary policy should cease when full employment is achieved.

7. The holding of substantial reserves is in any case likely to be limited to a few comparatively rich countries.

Why? Because the re-distribution of reserves among rich countries and the tendency of the concentration of reserves due to development from poorer to richer countries, stimulates it. This will, however, promote the development of poorer areas, and bring about an equalization of the rate of growth on the one hand and, on the other, contribute towards a minimization of the reserves required.

On the basis of the above reasoning, what is the best measure for solving the reserves problem? On this topic Balogh recommends an expansion of the conceptions of Bretton Woods. That is, the solution, for the reasons mentioned in 5 to 7 above, should combine in one organic measure a 'liquidity approach' (capacity for bringing about liquidity) and an 'equilibrium approach' (minimizing the need for liquidity). It would be sufficient to enlarge the functions of the 'Fund' and 'Bank' of the present Bretton Woods Agreements and require them to co-operate with each other. Unfortunately, however, there have been no instances of these organizations having co-operated to overcome those deficits in leading countries brought about by recessions.

First of all a reform of some of the basic principles of the IMF Agreement is necessary, giving it the character of a central bank, as follows :

Initially, it is necessary to change the character of members' subscriptions because, as the quotas under the present Agreement must be paid in gold to the extent of 25 per cent, this results in a decrease in the visible reserves of members. Even if a stand-by-credit is granted, this does not result in an increase in their reserves. In short, there is a defect in the relations governing subscriptions to the IMF, borrowings and repayments and the levels of the reserves of the members concerned. Could not this defect be eliminated by the following methods?

(*a*) To treat that part of the quota which is payable in gold (gold *tranche*) as part of the reserves of the member concerned. This is the first step.

(*b*) The second is to increase the gold *tranche* without additional gold payments.

(*c*) And lastly, to treat all deposits with the IMF as part of a member's reserves.

Next, the international central bank mentioned above should not only make ordinary loans, but should also effect positive open market operations so as to add to liquidity. Detailed regulations would of course be necessary to prevent the abuse of such powers. In order to make it easier for creditor countries to accept this proposal,

1. Voting power should be increased in step with increases in deposits. The qualified majority should also be raised in keeping with the degree of liquidity created, through which the raising of liquidity as a whole would naturally be controlled (because a certain number of votes are required for this).

2. Furthermore, it would be better for loans by the central bank to be limited by a formula of some kind (for example, by a certain ratio to the rate of economic growth or to external payments).

Balogh further proposes that the IMF set up an 'International Development Fund' which will allow it automatically to direct the increase in its permanent credit balances toward long-term investments in less-advanced countries, these investments having some connection with the economic activities or inactivities of advanced countries in order to reinforce the operations of the present World Bank. By so doing, the IMF could be expected to become an International Central Bank in the real sense of the term, and in addition the necessity to increase international liquidity would be lessened.

As the foregoing is a mere outline, a number of technical points have not been elaborated. These may be summarized as follows:

The first step involves the incorporation of the IMF's gold *tranche* into members' official reserves, an idea also to be found in the White Plan. It goes without saying that the present rule that drawings on the gold *tranche* are entirely automatic (see Chapter VI, section 4) should be firmly established.

As a second step, this gold *tranche*, that can be freely drawn upon, should be raised by members without additional gold payments. Increasing external payment facilities with no backing of gold in this way could be accomplished gradually.

The third step requires that the IMF should function as a 'Bank' both in name and in fact, with the result that the quota system would be abolished and a system of receiving deposits from members adopted; on the basis of these deposits, loans could be granted as is done by ordinary commercial banks. Further, the IMF would take positive steps to effect open market operations. Thus, the above deposits would represent an increase in the reserves of members. This proposal does not fundamentally change the current organization, as is clear from the fact that the 'Bank' is not required to issue new international currency. An increase in liquidity in that sense therefore is not possible, and the IMF cannot yet be considered as fully controlling credit. In this proposal also, the maintenance of the present dollar standard system is naturally an indispensable prerequisite.

What is most noteworthy in this proposal is that it aims at establishing a connection between short-term and long-term international credit, which is quite reasonable, if the Bretton Woods organization is to be transformed into a powerful international financial centre. The London and New York markets clearly show what an international financial centre should be. An error in its management, however, could confront it with the same danger that faces the two markets of 'making short-term borrowings and giving long-term loans'.

The positive reform mentioned above has also been proposed by Maxwell Stamp, a former adviser to the Bank of England and once a United Kingdom alternate executive director at the IMF and director of the Fund's European department. As previously mentioned, he made his proposal in the October 1958 number of *Lloyds Bank Review*. He repeated his proposal in *The Guardian* on 13 February 1961.[1] The gist of his proposal is as follows:

The IMF should issue gold guaranteed certificates, and members should agree to be ready to buy these with their own currencies. The IMF should, through an Aid Co-ordinating Agency, apportion these certificates among the poor and underdeveloped countries suffering from balance of payments difficulties due to their development plans. The countries receiving them would buy capital equipment from the advanced countries, which would then treat them as if they were gold, and could incorporate them in their reserves or use them for payments to other members. Their exchange into gold would only be permitted in special cases such as their being needed for payments to non-member countries. Countries such as the United States, which are prepared to sell and purchase gold at a fixed price, should have the option of handing over these certificates when asked to exchange a dollar balance for gold.

In this way, members with surplus reserves would automatically be able to use them to aid poor and underdeveloped countries, with the additional advantage that their reserves would suffer no real deterioration. More than that, they would be able to avoid the exchange risk that may accompany their foreign currency holdings. This proposal may in fact be said to be an adaptation of the gold note plan devised earlier by Keynes.

[1] Maxwell Stamp, 'The Fund and the Future' in *Lloyds Bank Review*, October 1958, pp. 1-20; 'Ending the World's Gold Shortage' in *The Guardian*, 13 February 1961. He revealed also his revised plan in 'Moorgate and Wall Street, Autumn 1962'. The feature of the new plan is the introduction of quotas of certificates that members should be ready to accept.

At first glance, it might be thought that, as it is designed to induce foreign countries which prefer gold to take up IMF certificates, there is not much difference between this plan and the Bernstein proposal; but there is in fact a great difference between them. In the Bernstein proposal, IMF debentures are merely bonds with a fixed term the redemption of which could only be demanded of the IMF, whereas in this proposal they are a new international currency of the same character as gold and capable of circulating freely between nations. Their issue, therefore, has the same effect as the international creation of gold and thus adds greatly to international liquidity. In view of this, great precautions should be taken lest they produce inflationary tendencies. Moreover, as their issue would strengthen the position of the IMF as a creator and controller of credit, their introduction would involve an important reform of the present Agreement. It is also noteworthy that while the Bernstein proposal aims at adjustment between key countries, this proposal is more interested in relations between advanced and less advanced countries.

In view of its character, therefore, this proposal is a somewhat drastic reform plan, but any increase of liquidity under it is of a limited nature [1] and it does nothing so fundamental as to abolish the dollar standard system itself.

The debatable point of this, as of the Bernstein proposal, is whether members who have a preference for gold can be induced to accept gold guaranteed certificates instead. Stamp is of the opinion that the basis of gold guaranteed certificates is not gold, and that the agreement among members to offer and receive them as if they were gold is sufficient for the purpose. It is not, however, clear that the matter is quite as simple as that.

This kind of reform plan brings us back to the theory of a flexible or floating exchange rate, for these arguments would

---

[1] Stamp presupposes the following cases: (*a*) Decline in the exports of countries producing raw materials. (*b*) Bad harvests of agricultural products. (*c*) Global depression.

He also makes the following suggestions to strengthen the IMF: (*a*) Abolition of the conditions for lending, as provided by the Agreement, Article V, Section 4. (*b*) Reinforcement of long-term finance by other organizations. (*c*) Promotion of the flow of private capital.

force a change in the present Agreement's principles regarding parities and fixed rates.

To avoid confusion some definitions will be helpful. A fixed rate means a rate that only permits such fluctuation as occurs in the gold standard system or within 1 per cent above and below the par value in the present Agreement; a flexible rate is one that, though it may go beyond the limits fixed above, still preserves certain limits for fluctuation.[1] A floating rate means a rate that is free to move without limits.

At the present time arguments for the adoption of flexible or floating rates, as a means of dealing with the international liquidity problem or of balancing international payments, are gathering force. Though it is desirable to examine those arguments to clarify the character of a monetary system, there is no space in the present volume to explore those discussions[2] which have taken place since the war as to whether fixed or floating rates constitute the better system. We shall, however, touch upon the main points of both and then outline recent developments. We shall then add some comments of our own to make clear their relation to the monetary system in general. Opinion as to which is best, a floating, flexible or a fixed rate, depends, as Lundberg says, upon the views taken upon the

---

[1] Though it is uncertain how large the margin of fluctuation should be, it seems that 3 to 5 per cent is usually thought to be suitable.

[2] As some examples of the discussions that have taken place, the following come to mind: 'What sort of Exchange Rates?' W. M. Scammell, *Westminster Bank Review*, May 1954. 'Flexible Exchange Rates', Sir Donald MacDougall, *Westminster Bank Review*, August 1954. 'Stable or Fluctuating Exchange Rates?' Per Jacobsson, *Skandinaviska Banken Quarterly Review*, October 1954. 'The Dilemma of Exchange Rate Policy', Erik Lundberg, *Skandinaviska Banken Quarterly Review*, October 1954. 'The case for Flexible Exchange Rates', F. A. Lutz, *Banca Nazionale del Lavoro Quarterly Review*, December 1954. 'Some Aspects of Convertibility', Gottfried Haberler, *Economia Internazionale*, February 1955. 'Fluctuating Exchange Rates and Convertibility', Weijo Wainio, *Kansallis-Osake-Panki Economic Review*, April 1954. 'Foreign Exchange Rate Theory and Policy', Arthur I. Bloomfield, *The New Economics* (Seymour E. Harris, editor). *Speculative and Flight Movements of Capital in Postwar International Finance*, A. Bloomfield, 1954. 'Fixed or Flexible Rate for Sterling?' *The Banker*, July 1955. 'Monetary Policy and External Balance', W. T. Newlyn, *Bankers' Magazine*, May 1955. 'Foreign Exchange Policy', R. F. Harrod, *Financial Times*, 19 July 1955. 'The Case for Variable Exchange Rates', J. E. Meade, *The Three Banks Review*, No. 27, September 1955. *International Monetary Policy*, 1957, W. M. Scammell. R. F. Harrod, *The Dollar*. (The Japanese version by the Economic Research Department of the Bank of Tokyo and published by the Jitsugyo-no-Nihonsha.) R. F. Harrod, *The Pound Sterling*. (The Japanese version by the Economic Research Department of the Bank of Tokyo and published by Shiseido.)

role of the price mechanism in solving the question of disequilibrium. Criticism of the current fixed rate system may be summarized as follows:

1. It is difficult to ascertain the correct rate.

   As has already been stated, the basic principles of parities in the IMF reflecting the objectives of an exchange equalization fund, were that stability is required to correct short-term instability, and flexibility to convert long-term imbalance, as Sir Roy Harrod says, but now that it is impossible to pursue this principle through freely fluctuating rates, it becomes merely 'an inanimate copy'.[1]

   That is, as it is difficult to judge whether or not an external imbalance is based upon a fundamental disequilibrium, there has actually been no experience of the above-mentioned IMF rule of lending stop-gap funds to deal with short-term disequilibrium and leaving a change of parity to solve a fundamental disequilibrium.

2. The present fixed rate system does not necessarily contribute toward the stabilization of exchange rates, for, (1), so long as there is any possibility of a change in parity, as under the current system, it is not conducive to a feeling of security, and therefore, unlike the fixed rate of the gold standard system, it has not even the advantage of ensuring the movement of long-term international capital, and (2) as there is always the possibility of one-way speculation based upon the expectation of a change in parity, there is the danger that the authorities concerned may be driven to a change in parity due to an accidental psychological factor.

3. The ideal of the IMF, 'controlled adjustment of rates', is an empty phrase, for, as a change of parity is generally known beforehand, orderly change is not to be expected. Moreover, as the authorities concerned are unable to decide on the equilibrium level in advance, they are apt to make a greater change than is necessary to avoid having to make a second change, the result being the possibility in the case of devaluation of causing a competitive lowering of rates.

4. This being so, there is the possibility that a change will be

---

[1] R. F. Harrod, *The Pound Sterling*. (The Japanese version published by Shiseido, p. 17.)

postponed to the last minute, thus allowing the case for the necessary change to gather force.

5. Speculators are capable of resorting to one-sided speculation and so, even if they are mistaken, they do not suffer any great loss, but if, on the contrary, their diagnosis is correct, they stand to gain enormous profits.

The above criticism in reverse will naturally illustrate the advantages of floating rates. They are as follows:

1. Under this system it is easier to determine the equilibrium level.
2. If a change of rates affects both exports and imports and thus automatically restores equilibrium, it is not necessary to hold large gold and foreign currency reserves; that is, this elasticity in rates can take the place of an increase in liquidity.
3. Exchange speculation in an opposite direction will have an effect on equilibrium and the point of equilibrium will be reached much sooner.
4. It becomes possible to institute independent domestic policies without being excessively influenced by balance of payments considerations.
5. The judgment of 'sharp-witted persons' (Meade's wording) is, generally speaking, more reliable and rational than that of monetary authorities.
6. A floating rate becomes a reliable indicator to the state of the balance of payments.

On the other hand the arguments against floating rates are based upon the following grounds:

1. Even if an exchange rate be altered, it does not necessarily mean the correction of an imbalance in payments, for at present elasticity of the supply and demand of exchange is very small. (Lutz, however, is sceptical about this 'elasticity pessimism', saying that its study, method and statistics are dubious. It may certainly be necessary to find a more perfect method.)
2. There cannot be a natural equilibrium rate.
3. The fixed rate governs domestic policies to some extent; that is, it is virtually a controlling power.

4. The floating rate imposes an exchange risk upon traders and thus hinders foreign trade.

   This risk can, of course, be transferred to speculators to some extent by forward exchange transactions, but it is undeniable that it imposes further expense upon traders. Though some contend that risks of this kind must exist under any policy, those they envisage are in most cases risks other than those connected with the foreign exchanges, such as a decline in national income or domestic prices, restrictions on trade and exchange, and the like.

5. What is called a wise judgment on the part of speculators, may not be reliable. There is no guarantee whatever that it will conduce to equilibrium. It is in most cases rather a disturbing element, for speculation invites speculation. Triffin says that though advocates of floating rates assert that information from speculators is reliable, yet if it be remembered that today all political and economic policies have their effect on exchange rates, the authorities should be credited with being better informed. They are indeed responsible for what they do, whereas speculators have no responsibility.[1] (Against this, those who are in favour of floating rates retort that destructive speculation is the result of other fundamental influences, for which it cannot be said that speculators are responsible.)

6. It obstructs international long-term investment. (At present, however, the psychology of investors is not influenced only by rate fluctuations. Even if fixed rates are maintained, it would not allay their apprehension — so runs one of the opposing arguments.)

7. If the exchange rate declines, it causes a rise in the prices of imported commodities, and this rise eventually extends to commodity prices in general. In turn this is reflected in the level of wages, thus nullifying the corrective effect on the balance of payments.

   That is to say, no matter whether the margins of fluctuation be large or a switch be made to entirely free, floating rates, the prerequisite must be the adjustment of policies in the country concerned, tending to correct any imbalance. If this is not so, it is impossible to avoid the vicious circle

[1] Robert Triffin, *Gold and the Dollar Crisis*, 1960, p. 84.

of a declining exchange rate leading to a rise in commodity prices and wages, or to expect an equilibriating effect from speculation; this is admitted even by advocates of floating rates. Obviously, even under floating rates, it is impossible to avoid deflationary policies.

8. There is no country today that can disregard the natural fluctuation of exchange rates. Those who favour floating rates, with few exceptions, expect to achieve equilibrium through an exchange equalization fund. If this fund is in continuous operation, then the margin of fluctuation will be considerably narrowed, but the advantages of automatic adjustment and economy in liquidity which are said to derive from flexible or floating rates would be lost.[1]

It was when the movement for the convertibility of currencies in Western Europe centring on the institution of the EMA became particularly active that the loudest arguments were heard for or against floating or flexible rates. At that time, Britain insisted upon the adoption of flexible rates, because it was very concerned about the effect that a restoration of convertibility might have on its balance of payments. Most of the continental countries on the contrary adopted a negative attitude for fear of the unfavourable effects that might result if sterling were in difficulties. As a result of a compromise, a degree of flexibility was introduced into rates, by the EMA, on condition that the margin of fluctuation was to be as moderate and as stable as possible. Contrary to general expectation, the flexible rate system was not, however, adopted after all, and convertibility was restored at the end of 1958. To the surprise of the IMF the liberalization of trade and foreign exchange created a much easier atmosphere, which affected capital transactions as well, and resulted in a plethora of hot money. It thus became questionable whether it would be possible to adhere to the principle of parity and achieve both internal and external equilibrium at one and the same time.

In the midst of this discussion, Professor J. E. Meade, who had been an ardent advocate of flexible rates, wrote an article

---

[1] R. F. Harrod in his *Anteiseicho-no Tsuka seisaku* (which is the Japanese version of *Policy against Inflation*, 1958, p. 56, translated by Takashi Murano and Michio Ebizawa and published by Shiseido, p. 61) says that under the floating-rate system the required amount of reserves will be higher.

entitled 'A plea for Flexible Exchange Rates' in the issue of *The Guardian* for 3 January 1961 and proposed the following approach :

1. The United States should stop selling gold.
2. The leading currencies, that is, the dollar, sterling, French franc and mark, should adopt flexible rates (which is used here in the same sense as floating rates) and should conclude a monetary agreement between themselves, making every effort to correct temporary imbalances with the aid of their exchange stabilization funds.

This approach is in effect a modern version of the Tripartite Agreement, and also a revival of the key countries approach.

On this same subject, W. M. Scammell, of the University College of North Wales, who is also an advocate of the flexible rate system, while showing sympathy with the basic idea of Meade's *Guardian* article, added a criticizing remark as follows :[1]

The Meade plan regards the conclusion of a monetary agreement among leading countries as very dangerous, in that it will result in the destruction of the IMF itself. It is better to keep the IMF in existence ; moreover, the United States would not permit its destruction. The following approach, therefore, is proposed :

1. The margin of fluctuation in exchange rates under the IMF Agreement should be expanded (the adoption of flexible rates being also considered).
2. Then an agreement should be signed providing for the setting up of exchange stabilization funds in the various countries and the co-ordination of their activities in foreign markets. In short, the proposed agreement is an agreement of limited scope, permitting a certain degree of fluctuation.

Scammell calls it 'a flexible rate system under the support of the IMF'.

Meade, in *The Guardian* of 23 January 1961, argues against this as follows :[2]

It is not the case that flexible rates rule out the IMF. It would be better to conclude a five-party agreement including

[1] W. M. Scammell, 'Flexible Exchange Rates', *The Guardian*, 7 January 1961.
[2] J. E. Meade, 'Exchange Rates and the IMF', *The Guardian*, 23 January 1961.

the IMF so that it may play the important role of a 'Supranational Equalization Account'. IMF should alsobe allowed to engage in market operations, both short-term and long-term.

Though it is not known whether these arguments had any effect, the central banks of eight West European countries (Belgium, Britain, France, Italy, Sweden, Switzerland, the Netherlands and West Germany) and the Federal Reserve System of the United States of America did, however, reach an agreement at Basle for the purpose of overcoming the disorder in foreign exchange markets following the revaluation of the Deutsche mark in March 1961. This was not an agreement, although it is usually called the Basle Agreement, the details of which have not been published. It is generally assumed, however, that it represents a version of the Meade-Scammell proposal without the provision of flexibility and is not markedly different from the Tripartite Agreement. *The Financial Times* thought highly of it calling it 'a silent revolution'.

Whether such a key country approach is durable and effective is debatable. To what extent will the signatories be able to buy and mutually support their currencies? For how long will they be able to guarantee amongst themselves adequate supplies of foreign exchange for their respective overbought positions? The Tripartite Agreement of former days, which was called a '24-hours gold standard', disappeared with the war; lack of space forbids discussion of it here. Nor can we fully assess the new proposal which is said not to lack supporters. Apparently the central banks in Western Europe, despite the agreement mentioned above, showed some hesitation after June 1961 about continuing to hold sterling balances. When Britain obtained a loan of $2 billion from the IMF it repaid the sterling balances held under this agreement, and this agreement was regarded as being only a stop-gap measure until Britain was granted the loan. So it may be asked whether it was right and proper to create a separate stabilization organization when the IMF system was already in existence.

The fact, however, that an agreement such as this was and is needed is one proof that the international control of currencies is of the utmost importance. The arguments for or against floating or flexible rates must be considered from this viewpoint.

As is shown by what has already been said, the exchange rate should not be regarded simply as the selling and buying price of a commodity. It is the ratio for the exchange of a country's currency and its maintenance is a national responsibility. Under the gold standard system the gold parity was the ratio for exchange and was automatically maintained with international co-operation. Following the collapse of the gold standard system countries established stabilization funds and endeavoured to secure control over currencies by international co-operation. When this was found to be impossible, they were obliged to resort to direct exchange control. The fixed rate system of the IMF eventually replaced the above measures.

The fact that rate fixing in this way is a kind of international control should not be overlooked. All central banks, therefore, even if they transferred to flexible or floating rates and possessed stabilization funds, would have had to agree secretly, in order to be realistic, on the conditions for intervention in exchange markets; otherwise there would be competition between the various stabilization operations. Thus a system of floating rates without international control is an adventure without precedent, and today, when international politics are so disturbed, it is impossible to think that this could succeed. Even if such stabilization agreements were to be concluded and were somehow successful, they would only serve to correct short-term disequilibrium, and would never constitute a fundamental solution of the question of international liquidity itself.

Section 4.—Suggestions for Fundamental Reform

The suggestions which have been mentioned, though differing in approach, are all designed to introduce that elasticity into the IMF system which at present it does not possess. In their attempts to solve the question of international liquidity, they are all transitional in nature and therefore not exhaustive.

Apart from these, however, there is a plan of a progressive nature directed to the fundamental reform of the Fund. This is the so-called Triffin Plan.

The Triffin Plan has had forerunners, one of which is the Stamp Plan which has already been mentioned. Another is that proposed by Sir Oliver Franks, Chairman of Lloyds Bank, in his annual statement for 1958. This plan advocates that the IMF should receive gold and foreign currency deposits, carry out international settlements by transfers in the gold accounts based upon those deposits and extend credit by granting overdrafts.

It was in two articles 'The Return to Convertibility, or Convertibility and the Morning After' and 'Tomorrow's Convertibility, Aims and Means of International Policy' in the March and June 1959 issues of the Quarterly Reviews of the Banca Nazionale del Lavoro that first expounded the Triffin Plan.[1] Furthermore, Professor Triffin made a report at the Elsinore meeting of the International Economic Association in April of the same year. He had also been asked to address the Joint Economic Committee of the American Senate and House of Representatives and his views suddenly attracted world-wide attention. With some additions these views were published in his book entitled *Gold and Dollar Crisis*, 1960. When Oscar L. Altman, adviser in the Research and Statistics Department of the IMF, criticized the plan in a long article on 18 October 1960,[2] Professor Triffin replied at once on the 21st of the same month, and also published an interim proposal to clarify the position.[3]

[1] Robert Triffin, 'The Return to Convertibility: 1926–31 and 1958–? or Convertibility and the Morning After', *Banca Nazionale del Lavoro Quarterly Review*, No. 48, March 1959. 'Tomorrow's Convertibility: Aims and Means of International Monetary Policy', *Banca Nazionale del Lavoro Quarterly Review*, No. 49, June 1959. *Gold and the Dollar Crisis: The Future of Convertibility*, 1960.
[2] Oscar L. Altman, 'Professor Triffin's Diagnosis of International Liquidity and Proposals for Expanding the Role of the IMF', 7 October 1960, IMF Staff Papers.
[3] The testimony of Professor Triffin in the United States Congress is given in detail in the following: Current Economic Situation and Short-run Outlook, Hearings before the Joint Economic Committee, Congress of the United States 86th Congress, Second Session, 7, 8 December 1960, by U.S. Government Printing Office.
The Arguments against and his interim proposal are given in the following: Robert Triffin, 'The Threat to the Dollar', *The Atlantic Monthly*, February 1961. 'International Monetary Crisis: Diagnosis, Palliatives and Solutions', *Quarterly Review and Investment Survey*. 'Altman on Triffin, A Rebuttal' in the above-mentioned U.S. Government publication.
Besides the above, Professor Triffin's arguments in English and French are given below: *Europe and the Money Muddle*, 1957. *The Future of the European Payments System*, (Wicksell Lecture), 1958. 'The Gold Shortage, The Dollar

Professor Triffin's ideas are based on the fact that hitherto international liquidity has been provided by an increase in the amount of gold and of international currencies such as the pound or the dollar, but that now no international financial centre can bear this burden; he argues that, although the disequilibrium in America's balance of payments may be corrected in a comparatively short space of time, a lack of liquidity will be keenly felt when this takes place and, therefore, that there exists an inseparable relation between liquidity and an international financial centre. He is therefore of the opinion that, as the existence of instability in the international financial field can be attributed to such a built-in de-stabilizer as the use of a national currency as an international currency, the question cannot be solved unless a fixed international currency be established and controlled by an international organization; to accomplish this the IMF system should be fundamentally reformed, and the Fund raised to the status of a world central bank.

To further his argument, Professor Triffin has analyzed and criticized the previously mentioned report by the IMF on 'International Reserves and Liquidity', and, after warning that the Fund was too pessimistic about the rate of growth of world trade (by estimating it at 3 per cent a year whereas he estimated it at 5 per cent), stressed that, in order to maintain this level, there should be a corresponding increase in liquidity. To meet this need what measures had been prepared? We shall see what Professor Triffin has to say about this below.

The nucleus of the Keynes Plan is that mutual settlements between all international authorities are conducted by transfers in the Bancor accounts opened with the Union.

The Triffin Plan is basically the same, beginning with member countries opening deposit accounts with the IMF, settlements being carried out by transfers between these accounts.

The suggestion is to impose upon members the obligation to deposit their gold and foreign currency reserves with the

Glut, and the Future of Convertibility', delivered at the Elsinore Meeting of the International Economic Association, August 1959. 'Improving World Liquidity', *The Banker*, January 1960. 'Le Crépuscule de L'étalon de change-or', *Problèmes Économiques*, No. 665, 27 September 1960. 'Restauration des monnaies européennes', *La Revue d'Économie Politique*, November-December 1960.

IMF to a minimum amount of 20 per cent (which will be adjusted automatically in keeping with an increase or decrease in these reserves) and thus provide funds for the deposit accounts. What should be noticed here is that this 20 per cent is the minimum considered necessary to operate the reform. Of course, members would be permitted to increase their deposits with the IMF beyond that limit. Professor Triffin also expects that those settlements reserves in foreign currencies which are at present held by members would be transferred into IMF deposits, except for some necessary working funds, for the reason that IMF deposits cannot be converted into gold so far as the compulsory portion (fixed at 20 per cent of gold and foreign currency reserves) is concerned; the excess over that limit, however, can be freely used for external settlements, or for conversion into gold.

The profits accruing to the IMF from advances or investments are to be apportioned among the members according to the size of their deposits with the IMF.

Further, as in the Keynes Plan, the Triffin Plan proposes that the IMF deposits should be expressed in terms of gold and their value should be stable. (Under the Keynes Plan, the value of unit 'Bancor' was not absolutely unchangeable.)

The reason why members prefer to hold the currencies of leading countries rather than gold as reserves is that not only is the cost of holding them lower than gold, but also that profits can be earned from investments in foreign government securities and the like. On the other hand, they might prefer gold to foreign currencies in order to escape the risk of changes in exchange rates or a suspension of convertibility. If, however, IMF deposits of the kind mentioned above were held as reserves, they would enable members not only to enjoy the advantages of holding foreign currencies as reserves, but also to avoid any of the drawbacks. With the adoption of such a system, Professor Triffin believes members will vest the greater part of their foreign currency reserves as deposits with the IMF. In this way, the disadvantages inherent in the gold exchange standard system will be removed; this is one of the principal aims of the Triffin Plan.

Assuming that foreign currency reserves are converted into IMF deposits and that the IMF permits their free convertibility into gold, how can the IMF maintain such convertibility? Dealing with this point Professor Triffin first analyzes the composition of IMF resources following its reform on the basis of the gold and foreign currency reserves of members held at the end of 1958. According to his hypothesis, of the free world's gold and foreign currency reserves at the end of that year, approximately $55 (U.S.) billion in all, about $11 billion would be transferred to the IMF as compulsory deposits. It is then expected that these deposits, other than those of the United States and Britain, would all be paid in foreign currencies, while those of the two countries mentioned would be paid largely in gold (as their reserves are held mostly in gold).

Thus, after the reform of the IMF its funds would consist of about $4.9 billion in gold and about $6.1 billion in foreign currencies (of which dollars would account for $3 billion, and sterling the equivalent of $2 billion).

As these would be compulsory deposits and would not be convertible into gold, no question would arise at this stage as to their convertibility, but Professor Triffin has in mind a division into two categories, that is, those showing an increase in deposits in the cases of the United States of America and Britain, and those reflecting an increase in the case of other countries.

As an example of the former, assume that demand increases for dollars and pounds in countries all over the world, as a result of which they buy these two currencies from the IMF against their deposits. As the IMF would credit these purchases to those two countries and thereby increase the amounts of dollars and pounds, their deposits would naturally go beyond their minimum limits giving those two countries the right of converting the excesses into gold. But the plan has laid down an important condition regarding such conversions. The condition is this: all the members have paid $3 billion in U.S. dollars and the equivalent of $2 billion in pounds sterling into their IMF deposits and, therefore, the IMF has total foreign currency claims of $5 billion against these two countries, and demands for repayment against the above credit at the annual rate of 5 per cent which amounts to $150 million in the case of the United States and to $100 million in the case of Britain; but until the $5 billion are repaid, the conversion into gold of the two countries' IMF balances would not be permitted.

Next, let us consider the case of an increase in the deposits of members other than the United States and Britain. This occurs when these countries, following Professor Triffin's proposals, voluntarily transfer their foreign currency reserves into IMF deposits above the minimum obligatory limit. According to Triffin's calculation, if members transfer all their foreign currency reserves into IMF deposits, then these will amount to $21 billion on the basis of balances held at the end of 1958. On the other hand, the gold reserves against these deposits being $4.9 billion, the percentage of IMF gold reserves against its total debts will fall below 25 per cent. Even in such a case, however, it is not expected that members will convert their balances into gold to any great extent. Not only that, but, as the above-mentioned 5 per cent repayment by the United States and Britain is expected to bring about an increase in gold amounting to $250 million a year in Professor Triffin's view convertibility into gold of the IMF deposits could be maintained to the extent required. Should any apprehension even then be felt, he considers that the following measures would be appropriate:

(1) The IMF should issue gold certificates with a good yield and an intermediate term, and request members to take them up, thereby blocking part of the excess deposits; and (2) the IMF should raise the minimum limit for the non-convertible portion of deposits from 20 to 30 per cent. It might be expected that those currencies, including the pound sterling, which at present are not officially convertible would be deposited with the IMF and be converted through that body. Against such a possibility, Professor Triffin proposes that so long as a country does not permit its currency to be converted into gold, the IMF should not permit its balances to be converted into gold.

Thus the IMF would create credit on the basis of these deposits, a principle in no way different from that of commercial banks anywhere. Commercial banks grant loans against funds they have received from their depositors and the funds thus lent are transferred to the accounts of the borrowers, bringing about an increase in their total deposits. The banks expand their advances on the basis of those deposits, which have been created by their advances. In this way, all commercial banks are able to create credit several times greater than the amount of the deposits initially received. The same would apply to the IMF after its reform. The IMF's advances would be made to those countries in need of funds on the basis of the above-mentioned minimum deposits. These advances would be transferred to the IMF deposit accounts in the name of the receiving countries. Should the receiving countries purchase the foreign currencies they need against these accounts, their accounts would be debited and the same amounts would be credited to the accounts of those countries which issued the currencies. Thus the IMF could increase its deposits by its own advances and thereby expand its base for credit creation so long as countries selling their currencies did not draw in gold on their IMF deposits. Therefore, the extent of credit that can be created by the IMF depends solely upon the total deposits that remain without being converted into gold. Professor Triffin would like to introduce a system whereby the currency of a country, after passing through the stage of a convertible bank note, becomes inconvertible, thus freeing itself from the bondage of gold and ultimately being capable of creating credit on an international basis. Though Triffin expects the IMF to create credit, he has in fact, imposed heavy restrictions upon this function so as to prevent global inflation. He proposes that in order to limit the creation of credit to an extent sufficient to meet the shortage of international liquidity, IMF advances should always be increased only in step with the rate of expansion of world trade and the increase in monetary gold, that is, by, say, 3 per cent this year and by 5 per cent next, thus eliminating the inflationary factor which might otherwise arise.

These advances, to countries in need, in keeping with the rate of expansion of world trade, would not be granted automatically as is the case with overdrafts under the Keynes Plan. These loans would require full agreement between the Fund and the member concerned, not only as to the maturity of the loan, but also as to the broad economic and financial policies to be followed by the member to ensure a long-run equilibrium in its international transactions without excessive recourse to trade and exchange restrictions. Lending by stand-by-credits is also permitted, as well as by another new method which allows an overdraft up to the minimum deposit limit by way of a stop-gap until approval is obtained for a definite loan.

All these forms of advances remain at the initiative of the borrowing countries. It is intended, however, that the IMF should at its own discretion buy securities on international markets and, through such open market operations, add to the amount of international liquidity. Moreover, it is also intended that it should invest its surplus funds in long-term finance through the IBRD.

To obtain a better understanding of the plan, some comments based on the explanation given by Professor Triffin are given below.

Why should the Triffin Plan begin with the deposits of members instead of with the automatic overdraft facilities as under the Keynes Plan? The reason is that under the Keynes Plan there is a danger of excess liquidity because of the creation of Bancor balances through the Union parallel with the existing international currencies. Further, the Keynes Plan is still unable to eliminate completely the dangers and defects inherent in the gold exchange standard system, whereas deposits under the Triffin Plan are designed to avoid this duplication by replacing existing gold and exchange reserves. As for the IMF, it creates international credit only in a non-automatic and deliberate fashion through the banking arrangements we have described.

Once members become familiarized with this new system, the amount of their voluntary deposits is expected to exceed the funds required by the IMF for its advances, and the compulsory deposits may thus be regarded as transitional. Though these compulsory deposits correspond to the quotas of the current system, they have two advantages over them. First they may be regarded as part of a member's reserves. Second, as the compulsory deposits are elastic in being based on members' trade and reserve positions, the volume of the IMF's reserves automatically reflects the level of reserves in the world as a whole. Where is the difference, then, between advances under the new and under the current system? The first difference is that under the new system the irrational regulation imposing restrictions upon currencies to be bought under Article V, Section 3 (*a*) (i), of the Agreement (that those currencies should be required for payments) is eliminated. Now that the convertibility has been restored, such restrictions are meaningless. The second difference is that under the current system, the convertibility of currencies depends chiefly upon the mechanics of the exchange market, so that transactions passed through the IMF involve simply the bilateral exchange of country A's currency for that of country B. This cannot be called truly multilateral. Under the new system, transactions and settlements through the IMF are literally multilateral and thus achieve perfectly the ideal contained in Article I, Section 4 (objective), of the Agreement.

In this connection, there has been much criticism of Triffin's arguments. First, in estimating the shortage of international liquidity, Professor Triffin made a simple, arithmetical calculation of the amount of reserves required as against the total value of world imports, and this invited criticism. This, however, was but his own analysis designed to obtain a general view, and reached in full awareness of the drawbacks of the quantity theory of money. Moreover, this method was employed in 1958 by the IMF itself in its noted report on 'International Reserves and Liquidity'.

According to Professor Triffin, the increase of international reserves has hitherto been financed (1) by an increase in the dollar and sterling debts of the countries concerned; (2) by the concentration of gold in the accounts of central banks; (3) by the change of gold parity; and (4) by sales of gold on the market by the Soviet Union. After the war, however, the greater part of the reserves (two-thirds in the last ten years) has been financed by (1). The world has now reached the stage at which any increase in dollar and sterling balances is not possible. Unless attempts are made to eliminate the built-in de-stabilizer which this represents, there may be permanent instability.

Second, the creation of the new international currency, which is the main object of the plan, ensures its conversion into gold, a feature which has aroused adverse comment. As is known, the instability of the current key-currency system cannot be removed immediately, for it depends upon the skill with which international credit is controlled, and if the creation of credit through the new currency results in a surplus of liquidity, then confidence in the new currency itself will be shaken and a general flight to gold will become a possibility.

On this point, Altman says that there are only two ways of eliminating the thirst for gold. One is to hold 100 per cent gold reserves and the other to provide for a one-way traffic in gold, as under the Keynes Plan. If requests for conversion into gold are met with insufficient gold reserves, stability will eventually come to depend upon the confidence reposed in the currency concerned. Though a flow of gold is troublesome, it is, after all, a naturally harsh disciplinarian. Can the new IMF effectively play the role of such a disciplinarian? That is, is there no contradiction between the short-term and the long-term stability of the exchange mechanism? As the new IMF is given the task of increasing liquidity, is not the above question especially appropriate? F. Hirsch has dealt with the same point. If, in accordance with this plan, members place foreign currency deposits with the IMF, he suggests that there is a danger that the United States or Britain may resort to restrictive payments policies, and to a reduction of their external assistance in order to reduce the deficits in their balance of payments. If so, international liquidity would be lessened instead of being increased. The reason why these two countries might resort to restrictive practices is that, under this plan, demands will be made for repayment in gold of dollar or sterling balances held by the IMF. This would therefore be very unfavourable to the United States and Britain, and would not prevent the eventual outflow of gold from the United States.

In reply to this criticism, Professor Triffin counters that his plan can never weaken the control of the flow of gold. All it does is to rectify the confusion of timing that arises under the gold standard system. Of course, it will not solve all the difficulties of control brought about by the movement of private short-term funds, for this solution remains in the hands of national financial authorities, but the new IMF is expected, by its advance and investment policies, to be in a more favourable position to contribute toward its solution. Further, says

Triffin, repayment in gold would be made in a gradual and deliberate manner, under the control of the IMF authorities, whereas under the current system, repayment of dollar balances can be demanded freely so that it is incorrect to assert that the position of the United States will be worsened. Some are optimistic as to the power of an international organization to control credit, while others are pessimistic. In this case, the arguments of the two sides may run parallel forever without ever being able to meet.

The third target for criticism is that under this plan the exchange rates of members' currencies are fully guaranteed. In order to give this guarantee, the IMF must conclude agreements with the members to ensure that debtor countries bear the exchange risk, should there be a change in the rate. Such an unlimited guarantee of the exchange rate is tantamount to saying that there will be no possibility of a devaluation. Indeed, it is quite unprecedented. If such guarantees could be given, the United States and Britain might even now be able to give a perfect exchange guarantee for their dollar and sterling balances.

This question of guarantees embraces a broad political problem. The United States and Britain both have not only liabilities in their own currencies, but assets as well in their external investments which are several times larger than their liabilities. Can they approve of a situation in which, while an exchange guarantee is demanded of them for their own currencies with the new IMF, yet none is received with respect to their credit balances in other currencies?

Triffin deals with this criticism. Such exchange guarantees, he says, are even now recognized for IMF transactions, and so they are not novel. Moreover, if the Agreement is to be carried out, it will lead naturally to such a practice. For example, IMF investments in U.S. Treasury bills are covered by a gold clause. This was also the procedure recognized in the European Payments Union (EPU); it is a more rational system than that in which the value of a credit may be reduced by an arbitrary devaluation on the part of a debtor country.

Generally speaking, the Triffin Plan has no clear-cut views regarding exchange rates and the stability of the gold value of the new currency. Nor is anything said about rates for market transactions, but in view of the fact that it is critical of floating rates, as mentioned above, it would seem to be based upon the fixed rate system.

However, it may be argued that, as under the plan, foreign currencies and gold reserves are to be replaced by the new currency, an exchange guarantee is absolutely necessary as an incentive, and is not therefore necessarily out of the question.

The fourth criticism of the plan is that the new system would create an imperfect international financial centre. What is more, this centre might exercise pressure on an existing monetary system such as the sterling area, obstructing its operations and even doing away with it altogether. It could also be said that the centralization of decisions on investments is extravagant and trouble-making. This criticism, however, is based upon a misunderstanding of the purpose of the new IMF system,[1] which, according to Professor Triffin, is designed to achieve a final adjustment between members by standing above such regional monetary systems. It should, in fact, be able to eliminate the dangerous features of existing regional monetary systems and conduce to their healthy management. He presupposes further that a new monetary area will be established among the West European countries on the lines of the OEEC. These regional systems are to play the role of provincial central banks with the IMF standing over them, to occupy the position now being held by the national central bank. Further, the formation of these regional systems means decentralization in putting IMF policies to work, and it is reasonable to expect them to mitigate the difficulties which the management of settlements by the IMF on a global scale would raise, and, especially, the investment of the enormous sums which would accrue to the IMF. Recognition of this should be on condition that they would be non-exclusive and would contribute towards the promotion of consistency and harmony amongst member countries.

Professor Triffin seems deliberately to avoid discussion of this matter. It would, however, seem natural that, if the management of the new IMF is carried out in an ideal fashion

---

[1] Professor Triffin, saying that he has never heard such criticism from British quarters, quotes from the following: Brian Tew, *International Monetary Co-operation*, 1945–60 (5th ed., London, 1960).

and its position as an international financial centre is reinforced, the existing centres should be under the IMF and their
prestige comparatively decline, for it is the aim of the new
IMF gradually to replace the reserves held in members'
currencies by the new international currency. Even allowing
for this, it will not necessarily be an evil from an international
point of view, except in the case of the United States and
Britain.

The fifth criticism is that the investments and advances of
the new IMF will be mostly of a capital nature and will be
made directly to underdeveloped countries, running the risk
of borrowing short and lending long, and thereby weakening
the liquidity of its assets. While recongizing the validity
of this criticism, Professor Triffin argues that long-term
investment in underdeveloped countries would not be made
directly, but indirectly through the purchase of World Bank
debentures and other securities. Further, they would be made
in existing financial centres such as Amsterdam, Frankfurt,
London, New York and Paris and, therefore, the lending
capacity of those centres would be reinforced. It is true that
this does not exclude the danger of 'short-term borrowings
and long-term lendings', and also that the IMF liabilities of
those centres may expose them to a flow of short-term, speculative funds. This, however, is a traditional danger faced by
such centres, and as the funds of the new IMF would gradually
increase in step with the increase in the reserves of member
countries, it would not experience a need to withdraw large
amounts of its investments from the markets of member
countries.

In addition, the ratio of compulsory deposits with the IMF
may be raised in case of necessity and this should constitute a
powerful dyke against such a danger. Even so, there might,
however, be some strain placed upon the IMF's reserves, as
compared with the present situation, if any attempt were made
to establish a connection between the flow of short-term funds
and long-term investment.

Taking all these arguments into consideration, none have
exposed any vital defect in the plan. Thus the question of
whether such a fundamental reform is necessary for the future
can now be discussed.

We ask, therefore, whether the proposed reform is necessary or possible in the near future. Most of the critics are of the opinion that it is still premature, and Professor Triffin himself recognizes this. That is why he has put forward an interim proposal to achieve his objective, progressively. Its main points are as follows:

The IMF should declare that it is at all times prepared to receive members' reserves as deposits,[1] which would bear an exchange guarantee and would earn interest. Further, these deposits would be automatically adjusted with changes in the levels of members' reserves. Under this system, the increase of deposits could be expected in most cases to provide a large excess of receipts over payments in the overall balance of payments, and therefore, the currencies concerned would be concentrated in those countries most in need of them for international settlements. Furthermore, these deposits, unlike the present quotas, could be mobilized to act as reserves for members without damaging their physical reserves, since they could be utilized for international settlements by mutual transfers whenever necessity arose. Professor Triffin, considering it practical to effect the intended reform gradually, proposes that further changes should be carried out step by step, and in close liaison with the financial authorities of member countries.

In this way, if the function of the IMF were gradually reinforced, it would contribute all the more towards the strengthening of international currencies such as the dollar and sterling. The U.S.A. and the U.K., if the IMF were to assume the great responsibility of controlling credit, could readily restore complete freedom in monetary and financial policies; that is, they would achieve simultaneously both external and internal equilibrium.

The advent of such a supranational financial organization, would, however, inevitably restrict members' financial sovereignty and their voting rights in the IMF, based upon the present system of quotas, would suffer a great change. The real obstacle to be surmounted, therefore, is not to be found in technical details but in profound political questions. It is also doubtful whether the administrative organs of the

---

[1] The acceptance by the IMF of these deposits has already been proposed by the Radcliffe Committee.

new IMF would be able alone to discharge their enormous responsibility on such a global scale. This is the reason why Professor Triffin contemplates the decentralization of the IMF's functions. He argues that future events will inevitably lead us to a fundamental reform of the current international monetary system. The question, therefore, is not whether these proposals will eventually be put into effect, but whether the free countries, before the development of very serious difficulties, will show enough wisdom and elasticity to adopt them.

Lastly, we must mention that there is another measure of attaining international liquidity, which does not resort to any of the foregoing procedures. It is that upon which Sir Roy Harrod has insisted throughout, namely, the raising of the price of gold. When his work, *The Dollar*, was published in 1953, his argument was directed chiefly to secure relief for the world economy, which at the time was suffering from a shortage of dollars. When, however, the worsening of the Americans' unfavourable balance of payments became pronounced, Harrod's point that this would help its international payments and would reinforce international liquidity took on added significance. Further support for this is to be found in Harrod's article entitled 'Wall Street and Gold' published on 22 June 1962 in *The Financial Times*. There he declares that as long as the United States does not raise the price of gold, it is bound to suffer a serious slump in Wall Street. He reasons along these lines: if the United States adopts low interest rates as its domestic economic policy, there will arise a difference between domestic rates and those of foreign countries, which in turn will result in an outflow of short and long-term funds and lead to a serious dollar crisis. The dilemma of a domestic slump or dollar crisis that now confronts the United States, he affirms, is the inevitable consequence of the ever-growing inadequacy of international liquidity. To solve the problem, expedients such as the Paris Club[1] or the Basle Agreement (perhaps even the Triffin Plan), may not be enough, and, he goes on to say that an increase of liquidity on a large scale will be required.

[1] The member countries which accepted to subscribe emergency funds for the IMF totalling $6 billion are called the Paris Club. They are Belgium, Britain, Canada, France, W. Germany, Italy, Japan, Sweden, Switzerland, the Netherlands and the U.S.A.

Harrod's contentions, generally speaking, are based on the foregoing analysis. The most noteworthy point, however, is his insistence that the raising of the price of gold is not merely aimed at an increase in the value of gold holdings but also that 'first, a rise in the price of gold would bring down interest rates all over the world and accordingly reduce the outflow of capital from the U.S.' and 'second, it would give a great boost to American exports', because, owing to the raising of the price of gold, not only the United States but also other countries 'would feel able to embark on a more expansionist policy'; this would bring about an increase in imports by all countries and a rise in the exports of the United States. By raising the price of gold, therefore, it would be possible, he reasons, to make a considerable improvement in the American balance of payments.

Considering that there is no possibility of the price of gold being raised in the near future, Sir Roy Harrod has recently suggested an alternative and practical plan, which can be summarized as follows :

(1) Members of the IMF should be entitled to utilize their drawing rights at their own discretion and these drawing rights should henceforth be called 'deposits'.

(2) Members would then be able to draw cheques upon the IMF within the outstanding balance of these deposits which it would be convenient to have denominated in the currency of the member countries. Thus conversion of one currency to another would be effected in the books of the IMF. The operation would not affect the size of the total liabilities of the IMF. These would be equal in amount to the sum of all quotas and would constitute a closed circuit.

(3) The national currencies now held by the IMF should be returned to their owners as no longer serving any useful purpose. This would be a mere book-keeping operation. In addition the Scarce Currency Clause and the General Arrangement for Borrowing should be rescinded. Under these arrangements the IMF would not need any gold, because members' deposits constitute a closed circuit and do not require convertibility into gold, but the gold held by the IMF and as subse-

quently added to, could be used to make loans to members in special balance of payments difficulties.

(4) The quotas in the IMF should be increased possibly by 6·5 per cent annually, for some years. The payment of 25 per cent of the added quota would be made by gold, and 75 per cent by National Certificate of Indebtedness.

(5) To generate sufficient confidence in the reserve currencies (at present the dollar and sterling) the following proposals are recommended :

(i) Establishment of a zero date.

(ii) At the end of one month establish (*a*) the size of (say) the U.S. reserve, and (*b*) the size of foreign holdings of (say) dollars.

(iii) If there are declines in both of these figures, compared with the status of the zero date, the IMF should open a line of credit in favour of the U.S.

(iv) The same procedure should be adopted at the end of every month. If there is a change in the need of the IMF loan, compared with the status at zero date, the line of credit should be altered accordingly.

(v) At the end of the third year, if a line of credit was still due, it should be repaid at the rate of 5 per cent a year over twenty years by (say) the U.S.

Section 5.—Conclusion

We have now to draw our conclusions from the opinions expressed and the suggestions that have been made. Whether a fundamental reform of the current system is necessary depends, after all, upon the prospects for the future of international liquidity. If we thoroughly examine the subject of international means of payment, we shall find that there are three facets. The first concerns liquidity; the second has to do with the centre of international finance; and the third, which is related to the above, regards the control of gold. Being closely inter-related, these facets should be discussed together, but for the sake of convenience we shall take them up one by one.

Let us first consider the question of liquidity. It is well known that Triffin's opinion on this topic is based upon his pessimistic judgment of the future. On the other hand, those who take the opposite view, the optimists, consider that it is possible to cope with the situation by strengthening the key currencies, and that there is ample room for this. The optimistic view expects that the future growth and strength of the economies of the key countries, coupled with the increase in monetary gold, will bring about a continuing increase in the key currency holdings, which will meet the requirements of an increase in the volume of world trade. On this view, therefore, there is no case for the creation by the IMF of a new international currency, but rather for the elevation of some of those key currencies, say, the mark, to the status of an international currency, and for the correction of the short-term imbalance between key currencies.

Based on this trend of thought are all the currency stabilization agreements reached recently among the important West European countries, the adherence of major countries to Article VIII, and the various proposals for reform made by the IMF authorities. It seems, therefore, impossible to regard such agreements and proposals as mere temporary expedients.

With regard to the future of liquidity, however, a careful examination must be made free of all traces of careless optimism. The question of aid to emerging countries must also be taken into consideration, for it is highly questionable whether even the combined total strength of the key currencies will be sufficient to promote rapid growth in a balanced world economy. In other words, the speed of the economic growth of key countries must not be over-estimated. Moreover, in practice, the extent that such a currency as the mark can be utilized as an international currency in the future is doubtful.

Adequate consideration must also be given to the deflationary bias in the current system. To elaborate this: the current system does not automatically allow creditor countries to take measures to remedy an imbalance; so that there is a danger that the gold concentrated with them will be sterilized and thus exert pressure upon liquidity, while the effects of stringent monetary policies taken by debtor countries will tend to spread to creditor countries too, from which must come a contraction of trade on a world-wide scale.

Let us now assume that the question is limited to the nature of the international financial centre. The Triffin proposal presupposes that the IMF would become a strong centre over all others. There are some, however, who are opposed to this suggestion, mainly the present IMF staff, who are of the opinion that the world is not in need of a new centre, and consider that the existing centres, such as London and New York, are sufficient for the purpose. It is further contended that centres in the plural rather than in the singular are to be preferred. The reason given for this, for example, by Bernstein, is that if only one currency is used by all countries as a reserve, gold is the only means of flight from that currency, but if two currencies are utilized for this purpose, then the flight from one is merely a flight to the other. In consequence, the only problem is for these two centres to take measures to strengthen each other. Here again the underlying concept is that of the key countries approach. F. Hirsch also points out that it is not necessary to separate the two functions of national and international currency which are now being fulfilled by sterling and the dollar, and that it is easier to bring about the stabilization of those two currencies and thus add strength to their international credit. His reasoning stands in sharp contrast to that of Professor Triffin. These arguments are not free from contradictions. If a plurality of centres were so desirable as he argues, then it would be much more desirable for the IMF to be strengthened so that there might be yet another centre to co-operate with those already in existence.

All these arguments, however, disregard the historical fact that the gold standard system worked smoothly owing to the existence of a strong London centre, which unified the whole; and that those monetary systems, including the IMF, which were established after the last war, have functioned with no serious hitch, thanks to the existence of a powerful New York centre. True, there was monetary confusion during the 1930s, but it was partly due to the fact that at that time there were a number of centres, which were not sufficiently strong one against the other (see p. 154).

In order to do away with this confusion, the Tripartite Monetary Agreement was signed to allow for mutual assistance, but this attempt was killed by the last war; there was not even time to discuss its usefulness. Now, as previously mentioned, the Basle Agreement has again launched a similar plan, but it is too early for us to pass judgment as to whether it will succeed or not. Apart from this, if an optimistic view regarding liquidity is not warranted, it is also not desirable that there should be a number of strong centres. Such being the case, is it not natural, in the light of past performance, for us to desire that there should be only one genuine centre acting as a strong international organization?

The question of an international currency system must be considered in the light of the need to control gold, because it is impossible to disregard the existence of gold as a basic medium for international settlement. If, indeed, we could disregard gold altogether, then it is not too much to say that there would be no problem at all. In order to ensure the stabilization of international payments, therefore, the control of gold somewhere is a necessity. There was a time when this control was centred in London. It has since been removed to New York. It is entirely due to the fact that the United States has assumed such control that the IMF system at present does not include a complete control of gold. This being so, the current IMF system cannot be a self-sufficient currency system *per se*, and its role as an international financial centre can only be supplementary. To strengthen the IMF for the future, therefore, it must improve its control over gold. It was because he recognized this that Professor Triffin, in advocating a new international currency, posed as a condition convertibility into gold without resort to any Keynesian idea of inconvertible paper-money. Triffin's proposal, therefore, as he himself maintains, may be said to be more practical than that of Keynes.

If, however, going a step further, it aims at a thorough-going control of gold, the IMF may have to concentrate and distribute gold in a more positive manner than is intended in the Triffin proposal. And if this control is carried out effectively and, as a result, a system of settlement through a new currency proceeds smoothly and confidence in that currency increases, then gold may flow into the IMF more quickly than it flows out, and, as a result, come to be concentrated there. This process may be likened to that of convertible bank notes being issued by any central bank, giving place later to inconvertible paper money, with gold being thus concentrated in the central bank. If things develop in the way described, then gold may have to abdicate its status as an international currency. So long as the present situation persists, where gold is divided between several countries and is regarded as a measure of economic power, it may be impossible to dethrone gold from its status as an international currency.

In brief, we should not neglect the control of currency internationally, any more than we should nationally. And any international control of currency should, in practice, be through an international organization. Indeed, it is worthy of praise that the IMF, which began functioning against a background of a serious dollar shortage, has since been able to cope with the change of circumstances, by not adhering to formal agreements and by adopting flexible policies in management, in the midst of an ever-shifting world-wide economic structure; but if we ponder over the questions of liquidity, control of gold and the character of an international financial centre which underlie the international currency system, we cannot but feel the keen necessity of a fundamental reform of the current IMF system, not only for the short run but also for the long-term benefit of the international monetary organization.

Lastly, and with reference to the above system, there will naturally arise the question of relations between the free world and the Communist countries. As is well known, the present IMF was formed as part of the organization of the United Nations, and there was no intention of excluding the Communist world. However, no country behind the Iron Curtain is at present a member, and the IMF functions exclusively as a currency system among nations of the non-Communist world. It may not be amiss, therefore, to hope that with the establishment of peaceful co-existence between the two groups in the distant future, an international currency system may be formulated which would also include the Communist countries. But if there is no such possibility and the separate international currency systems of the two groups remain, the question then will be how to combine these two systems into a global organization.

EPILOGUE

FURTHER developments have taken place in the field of international foreign exchange since this book was written. These can be summed up as follows:

Since the Sixteenth General Meeting of the IMF held in 1961, the United States has taken a greater interest in the foreign exchange market. As a matter of policy, the United States had long made a point of exchanging foreign-held dollar balances for gold at the fixed price of $35 an ounce. Other countries, for their part, endeavoured to stabilize their rates against the dollar by operations on the foreign exchange market.

While others were active in this field, the United States was not, until ominous events — the rise in October 1960 in the market price of gold, the March 1961 revaluation of the Deutsche mark, the outflow of short-term funds from the United States giving rise to apprehensions about the dollar, and, much more serious, the adverse U.S. balance of payments — induced the U.S. Treasury Stabilization Fund to operate in the international exchange market early in 1961. The Federal Reserve System, too, began market operations on its own account in February 1962.

Obviously, a common principle governing the leading West European countries and the United States is essential if world-wide exchange operations are to be carried on with benefit to both. This is exactly what is now taking place. The United States is raising needed foreign currency by swap arrangements with the central banks of other countries. By this method the Federal Reserve Bank acquired foreign currencies up to September of 1962 to an equivalent of $700 (U.S.) million. Details are given in the table overleaf.

Thus the major countries have developed a new currency raising swap technique; while laudable as a means of re-inforcing international liquidity, and welcome as another type of key currencies approach, its effect is not likely to be more

FEDERAL RESERVE RECIPROCAL CURRENCY AGREEMENTS

Other Party to Agreement	Amount (in millions of dollars)	Date (of original agreement)	Term (in months)
Bank of France	50	March 1, 1962	3
Bank of England	50	May 31, 1962	3
Netherlands Bank	50	June 14, 1962	3
National Bank of Belgium	50	June 20, 1962	6
Bank of Canada	250	June 26, 1962	3
Bank for International Settlements	100	July 16, 1962	3
Swiss National Bank	100	July 16, 1962	3
German Federal Bank	50	August 2, 1962	3
Total for all banks	700		

Source: Federal Reserve Bank of New York, *Monthly Review*, October 1962.

than temporary. Liquidity will thereby be only moderately improved.

In this connection a noteworthy proposal was made in May 1962 to expand international liquidity in the future by Robert V. Roosa, Under-Secretary of the Treasury for Monetary Affairs, by a multi-reserve currency system. Though it is now holding foreign currencies under swap arrangements, it was suggested that the United States should go a step further and for the future should hold a considerable part of its reserves in the form of foreign currencies. The proposal also implied that after sufficient foreign currency reserves have been accumulated, the United States would not insist on dollars being used for settlement purposes, but would be willing to receive payments in other foreign currencies as well.

Even in debit, the United States would settle in dollars to a reasonable extent, and, in so doing, increase the world settlement reserves as a whole, irrespective of whether the U.S. payments position was in credit or in debit.

This multi-reserve currency system is noteworthy; but it is doubtful to what extent the United States and other countries would agree to include currencies other than the U.S. dollar and the pound sterling.

Meanwhile another scheme has taken shape to prevent speculative changes in price on the London gold market. The central banks of leading West European countries and the

United States have formed an international gold pool. The gist of the scheme seems to be that with gold funds subscribed on a quota basis, reportedly totalling $270 million, the Bank of England should stabilize the price of gold on the London market; this is, in effect, international management.

The *raison d'être* of the scheme is that the price of gold should be controlled internationally, rather than by the United States or Great Britain, as up to now.

This co-operative arrangement is now being put into practice on a modest scale, and as time goes on may develop into an authoritative organization actually able to stabilize gold on an international scale.

This scheme indeed has its merits; but what is there against the handing over of this control of gold to the IMF? Is it not that body which we wish to transform into the dynamic international financial organization of the future?

Still to be mentioned is the proposal made by Mr. Reginald Maudling, the British Chancellor of the Exchequer, at the IMF General Meeting held in Washington in 1962. In his speech he outlined a plan to increase international liquidity and proposed that:

1. The leading trading countries of the world should open *mutual* currency accounts with the IMF.
2. Any participating country in possession of surplus foreign currencies should deposit them in that account.
3. A gold guarantee should be attached to the balances in that account.
4. Any of these balances should be able to be used for re-purchasing a country's own currency when it is in deficit, and, in consequence, has its own currency deposited in the account.

If put into operation, the Chancellor's plan would at once lighten the burden hitherto borne by the United States and Britain as leading reserve currencies, and at the same time would make more easily available the supply of international settlement currencies to all countries. Further, countries holding U.S. dollars or pounds sterling would not have to run the exchange risks that accompany the holding of foreign currencies. Though the balances that the Chancellor speaks of would not at the outset be utilized for ordinary international settlements, yet there is a possibility of their developing into international currencies freely transferable between countries like gold. We can regard the proposal as one presaging the creation of an international central bank.

INDEX

Index

THE END